Questions
OF THE SOUL

Questions

OF
THE

SOUL

ANSWERS

FROM THE

BOOK
of
MORMON

DAVID A.
CHRISTENSEN

CFI
AN IMPRINT OF CEDAR FORT, INC.
SPRINGVILLE, UTAH

This is not an official publication of The Church of Jesus Christ of Latter-day Saints. The opinions and views expressed herein belong solely to the author and do not necessarily represent the opinions or views of Cedar Fort, Inc. Permission for the use of sources, graphics, and photos is also solely the responsibility of the author.

ISBN 13: 978-1-4621-1164-0

Published by CFI, an imprint of Cedar Fort, Inc., 2373 W. 700 S., Springville, UT 84663
Distributed by Cedar Fort, Inc., www.cedarfort.com

LIBRARY OF CONGRESS CATALOGING-IN-PUBLICATION DATA

Christensen, David A., 1949- author.
Questions of the soul : answers from the Book of Mormon / David A. Christensen.
   pages cm
ISBN 978-1-4621-1164-0 (alk. paper)
1. Book of Mormon--Commentaries. 2. Book of Mormon--Authorship. I. Title.

BX8627.C493 2013
289.3'22--dc23

2012050334

Cover design by Angela D. Olsen
Cover design © 2013 Lyle Mortimer
Edited and typeset by Emily S. Chambers

Printed in the United States of America

10 9 8 7 6 5 4 3 2 1

CONTENTS

CONTENTS

INTRODUCTION

Have you ever tried to assemble something like a toy or a prefabricated piece of furniture, or tried to install some high-tech machine without instructions? How about assembling a thousand-piece jigsaw puzzle without having the picture of the finished artwork to use as a pattern for your efforts?

It is safe to say that most of us, at some time or another, have experienced a situation like this. I have been accused more than once of recklessly attempting to assemble an object without a careful review of the instructions provided by the engineer or designer. I have often done pretty well at putting things together without a serious attempt to read, understand, and apply the assembly instructions. However, I remember one Christmas Eve, while taking on the role of Santa's Elf, I began the assembly of a riding toy for one of our small children. It looked easy enough! I smugly began to erect the toy, putting the axel in its proper place, installing the wheels where they obviously went, screwing on the nuts, and finally tapping the little, decorative hubcaps exactly where they were supposed to be. *There*, I thought. *Completed, done, and ready to be placed beneath the lighted Christmas tree with the wrapped gifts.*

"Oh," I said to my wife, who was busily working on the less compli-cated project of filling the festive Christmas stockings. "Now, a big, red, festive bow attached to the shiny handles, and I'm ready to take on the next serious project." As I cleared the clutter of the box and other trash associated with the packaging of the now-assembled toy, I noticed two small, round pieces with holes in the middle (washers) lying on the carpet floor. Confused, I began to wonder where those pieces were sup-posed to have been included in the project just completed. I muttered, "Surely these are just extra pieces!" Then, in an effort to save face with my wife—who was quite successfully finishing filling the stockings—I silently said to myself, *Are these two little pieces really all that important to the functionality of that toy, which seems to be ready for riding on Christmas morning?* It was then that I consulted the instruction manual and dis-covered where those two small, seemingly insignificant pieces were to be placed in order to avoid improper wearing out of moving parts. A time-consuming, humiliating, and somewhat-frustrating effort to dismantle the toy ensued. The corrections were made, and the toy was ridden by more than just one of our eight children for what seemed to be more than 100,000 miles before it was donated to Deseret Industries and pos-sibly driven for another 100,000 miles.

Somewhat like the instruction manual for the toy, the Book of Mormon is the best handbook for living—given by a loving Father to His children. Referring to it daily will help us discover the missing parts that we don't even know are missing until we start to put the boxes and wrappers away. Like the instruction manual I consulted to find the cor-rect placement of those two little, metal washers, this book of books can help us find the missing parts in our lives—then find the answers of what to do to correct our mistakes or to find more fulfillment in making those corrections.

I invite you to look at the Book of Mormon from a different per-spective than you have in the past. We (members of the Church of Jesus

Christ of Latter-day Saints) know that an angel delivered an ancient record of the inhabitants of the American continent (inscribed on metal
plates of gold) to the young man Joseph Smith, who translated those
plates by the gift and power of God. It's possible, even probable, that
in that simple understanding, we can forget something very basic that
renders the Book of Mormon even more powerful than we think. That
understanding comes from remembering how it was written and what
the book really is. It's neither a history book nor a doctrinal reference
document. It was not written to inform us of historical, geographical,
or social conditions or cultural insights—although it can give us hints
of each.

Imagine for a moment that you walk into a library. There are
shelves with books and periodicals organized in a fashion that allows
you, a reader, to look at history, geography, science, and current affairs.
Do you have that image in your mind? Now, go back in time many
centuries. You walk into another room, perhaps a large cavern or a cave.
As you look closely, you see that in this room are stacks and stacks of
metal plates, perhaps with an occasional leather or other material rolled
up scroll-like. There is definite organization of the library, and you are
awestruck. With that image in your mind, now visualize a man (who
lived three-plus centuries after the advent of Christ upon the earth) going into that library by divine decree with a mission.

His name is Mormon. He takes on the vocation by divine errand to
read and pull from the entire collection—making a smaller, condensed
version containing quotes from those books, threads, and patterns, and
from his own commentary from time to time. Can you imagine that
responsibility? Is it within your own capability to consider such a for-
midable task? Mormon does take on that task. It will take him years to
do, and in the end he will run out of time and pass on the task of finishing the work to his son, Moroni. Remember too that he has no word-
processing programs or keyboards or voice-command devices by which

to dictate his work. No. It's stylus and metal etching all the way—pure labor just to write, let alone to read and extract important information.

Let's take a look at Mormon's own words as he works through the process. Beginning with the end of his writing can help us establish a pattern. In about AD 385, just before he concludes his work that constitutes the majority of the book, he explains to us readers what he's tried to accomplish. He says of his experience in condensing a library of plates into a single volume—

The Words of Mormon 1:5–7	Commentary:
5 Wherefore, I chose these things, to finish my record upon them, which remainder of my record I shall take from the plates of Nephi; and I cannot write the hundredth part of the things of my people.	*He writes to us in simple terms we can understand . . . "listen up," he seems to say. "I can't give you future readers even 1 percent of this library!"*
6 But behold, I shall take these plates, which contain these prophesyings and revelations, and put them with the remainder of my record, for they are choice unto me; and I know they will be choice unto my brethren.	*He reminds us as we read that he has taken those things that he feels to be important, knowing full well that they will be of importance to those who follow him . . . as his brethren and future readers of the book.*
7 And I do this for a wise purpose; for thus it whispereth me, according to the workings of the Spirit of the Lord which is in me. And now, I do not know all things; but the Lord knoweth all things which are to come; wherefore, he worketh in me to do according to his will.	*Mormon indicates that all he has done in making the compilation has been done by the influence of the Spirit. He reminds us that he really doesn't know everything. But the Lord does, and he has tried to write according to the will of the Lord.*

Now let's look at his words in Helaman 3:13–15. Remember, this is the Book of Mormon! We can say that almost everything in the entire Book of Mormon was either written by Mormon or "cut and pasted" from the library of plates. Mormon is pulling stories and things written during the time of Helaman, but it is important to remember that these words are of Mormon (not Helaman), who is commenting on what Helaman did and wrote about.

Helaman 3:13–15	Commentary:
13 And now there are many records kept of the proceedings of this people, by many of this people, which are particular and very large, concerning them.	*Mormon reminds us that the library is big and full of lots of records.*
14 But behold, a hundredth part of the proceedings of this people, yea, the account of the Lamanites and of the Nephites, and their wars, and contentions, and dissensions, and their preaching, and their prophecies, and their shipping and their building of ships, and their building of temples, and of synagogues and their sanctuaries, and their righteousness, and their wickedness, and their murders, and their robbings, and their plundering, and all manner of abominations and whoredoms, cannot be contained in this work.	*Again he emphasizes that he can't give us even 1 percent of the library. He says there's so much! There are records about wars and contentions, building ships, constructing temples and meeting houses, the good days and the bad days, sexual sin, and more. Mormon says in simple terms, "I can't give you much!"*
15 But behold, there are many books and many records of every kind, and they have been kept chiefly by the Nephites.	*Again he declares that the collection of plates is a Nephite one, with just a few others sprinkled in (like brass plates and a record found by a Nephite search party a few hundred years previous).*

Can you imagine the library? So many records! Mormon is restricted in the amount he can write. His pattern of speech and description follows the concept that he cannot give to us, the future readers, very much of the whole library—not even 1 percent!

Let's look at a few more of Mormon's words. The time frame is now just a couple of decades before the birth of the Savior. Mormon is in a particular section of the library that covers about twenty-five years. To put that into perspective, he's trying to extract important information covering about the life span of a young returned missionary. Twenty-five years isn't long. Let's read.

3 Nephi 5:8	Commentary:
8 And there had many things transpired which, in the eyes of some, would be great and marvel-ous; nevertheless, they cannot all be written in this book; yea, this book cannot contain even a hun-dredth part of what was done among so many people in the space of twenty and five years;	*Mormon seems to say, "Out in the future, someone familiar with my day is going to say, 'Mormon, how could you have left out those stories and teachings in that part of the library?' They might continue by saying something like, 'You got some of the good stories in, but how could you have left out the one about . . .'" Then, once again, Mormon asserts in certain terms, "I can't give you even one percent of twenty-five years either—there's just not room!"*

Are we seeing the pattern? Again Mormon reminds us that he's not compiling a short history, nor is he trying to fill in gaps; he's simply giv-ing us what the Spirit of the Lord impresses him to relate. Now, let's go to a just a few years later, after the Savior has visited the Americas and ascended. He was on the American continent for days—perhaps weeks. But relatively speaking, it was a very short time.

3 Nephi 26:6	Commentary:
6 And now there cannot be written in this book even a hundredth part of the things which Jesus did truly teach unto the people;	*One more time, Mormon says in so many words—"I can't even give you 1 percent of a week or two . . . just days in fact.*

Christ gave us so much in such a short time. The pattern is set, and the way of describing the challenge is articulated by simply saying that the library of plates is far too vast to try to include more than the most vital of records. Careful decision making on what to include and what to leave out is the only way Mormon can give us one book—instead of a mini library of books!

Let's take a look at one more scripture that can help us to understand how the product of the Book of Mormon is so wonderfully tailored to our needs.

Mormon 8:1, 34–39	Commentary:
1 Behold I, Moroni, do finish the record of my father, Mormon. Behold, I have but few things to write, which things I have been commanded by my father.	*Notice the time has come when Mormon will no longer write, and his son, Moroni, is going to finish up the record.* *Before he does, however, he will go into the library and do much the same as his father. He will take one volume of plates (found by a search party on an expedition centuries earlier) and sort through that voluminous history covering 1,900 years, condensing it to just fifteen short chapters (the Book of Ether). He states, just as his father did, that he can't give even 1 percent of that history (see Ether 15:33).*

34 Behold, the Lord hath shown unto me great and marvelous things concerning that which must shortly come, at that day when these things shall come forth among you.

He says, "I've seen a lot of what's going to occur in your day."

35 Behold, I speak unto you as if ye were present, and yet ye are not. But behold, Jesus Christ hath shown you unto me, and I know your doing.

"In fact," he says, "I've seen you, in your day, and I know what you struggle with yourselves. It is Christ Himself who has shown you to me.

36 And I know that ye do walk in the pride of your hearts; and there are none save a few only who do not lift themselves up in the pride of their hearts, unto the wearing of very fine apparel, unto envying, and strifes, and malice, and persecutions, and all manner of iniquities; and your churches, yea, even every one, have become polluted because of the pride of your hearts.

"We know you, and we know that you struggle with the external—your clothes and your money. You also neglect the poor. You are so focused on 'things' and are so distracted by your 'world.' You are obsessed with comparing yourselves to each other."

Think about it. Mormon and Moroni were experts in seeing that the seed of pride is comparison. The one, visible way to give ourselves a "quick fix" for our need for comparison is to show that we have money, things, and fine clothes of the brand somehow selected by those few at the top of the heap.

37 For behold, ye do love money, and your substance, and your fine apparel, and the adorning of your churches, more than ye love the poor and the needy, the sick and the afflicted.

38 O ye pollutions, ye hypocrites, ye teachers, who sell yourselves for that which will canker, why have ye polluted the holy church of God? Why are ye ashamed to take upon you the name of Christ? Why do ye not think that greater is the value of

"Praise of others and where you stand on the ladder of success are so important to you that you seem ashamed of the fact that you are Christians who have taken upon yourselves Christ's name."

an endless happiness than that misery which never dies—because of the praise of the world?

39 Why do ye adorn yourselves with that which hath no life, and yet suffer the hungry, and the needy, and the naked, and the sick and the afflicted to pass by you, and notice them not?

40 Yea, why do ye build up your secret abominations to get gain, and cause that widows should mourn before the Lord, and also orphans to mourn before the Lord, and also the blood of their fathers and their husbands to cry unto the Lord from the ground, for vengeance upon your heads?

To end, Moroni asks a series of questions that are calculated to get us to examine our hearts and motives.

SUMMARY

Mormon and Moroni saw our day! The only way they knew what to include in the 1 percent they gave to us in the Book of Mormon (and why they left out the 99 percent, which still remains in the darkness of the library) is that they saw our day and were inspired to include only what we would need.

Therefore, we have in the Book of Mormon the greatest handbook for living—a book written for our day, for us! This handbook is the basis for answers to the "questions of our souls" as we live-out in the twenty-first century what they saw in the third century. In the Book of Mormon, we read what they were inspired to select from the library—a library that began as early as twenty-plus centuries before Christ (the Jaredite history) and spanned through the sixth century (before Christ) to the fourth century (after His birth). The Book of Mormon is the "handbook of handbooks," which can direct and give answers to the questions of our souls.

In comparing the Book of Mormon to an instruction manual, we need to be careful to remember at least one big difference. While the assembly instructions of the aforementioned toy provided a step-by-step approach to put one specific gadget together, the fascination with the Book of Mormon is that it is wonderfully universal and applies to so many situations. I have noticed over the four-plus decades of my life, from my later adolescent years to the present, that the principles taught in the Lord's instruction to us in The Book of Mormon have applied universally. My struggles with peer pressure as a teenager were different than the concerns I had as a young missionary in Mexico. Feeling concern over an impending draft into the military, courting my future wife, and later starting our family as a newly married couple were certainly different than many anxious days as a bishop, unsettled nights as a stake president, or times when, of necessity, I had to draw upon the powers of heaven as a mission president to help a struggling missionary through troubled waters. The answers to the questions associated with each distinct era of our lives—and the lives of those we love and serve— are caringly provided by our Heavenly Father in the stories Mormon and his son, Moroni, were inspired to include from the library of plates. Answers are found in carefully selected accounts ranging from Nephi to Alma, Korihor to Gidgiddoni.

Since the Restoration of the gospel of Jesus Christ upon the earth, prophets have taught of the importance of the Book of Mormon in the lives of its readers.

The Prophet Joseph Smith—who not only lived great, but also died as a witness of the truthfulness of his work and role in bringing The Book of Mormon forth—stated with boldness that "I told the brethren that the Book of Mormon was the most correct of any book on earth, . . . and a man would get nearer to God by abiding by its precepts, than by any other book" (Introduction to the Book of Mormon). That promise alone will give any answer-seeking person a pathway to find solutions, obtain solace in a troubled world, and plan a better orientation to navigate through a modern society handicapped by a gyrating moral compass.

We can find answers to questions on almost any subject on the information highway of the Internet, with volumes stored in some nebulous cloud library in cyberspace. However, one must still sift through it all to find out what is the truest and best answer to whatever their question. The Book of Mormon is not only the most correct of any book on earth, but it also promises to be a source to the answers of the questions of the soul. Its stories are filled with divine perspective that can tutor troubled minds and bid its reader to consider tried and tested formulas based on prophetic teachings. The book is, quite simply, the most adequate handbook for living in existence today—with engaging examples of those who lived according to divine direction and prospered and those who rejected divine direction and suffered.

Ezra Taft Benson taught that the Book of Mormon answers the great questions of the soul and that we must flood the earth with this great book:

> I challenge our mission leaders to show their missionaries how to challenge their contacts to read the Book of Mormon and pray about it. Missionaries need to know how to use the Book of Mormon to arouse mankind's interest in studying it, and they need to show how it answers the great questions of the soul. Missionaries need to read with those they teach various passages from the Book of Mormon on gospel subjects.
>
> I have a vision of homes alerted, of classes alive, and of pulpits aflame with the spirit of Book of Mormon messages.
>
> I have a vision of home teachers and visiting teachers, ward and branch officers, and stake and mission leaders counseling our

people out of the most correct of any book on earth—the Book of Mormon.

I have a vision of artists putting into film, drama, literature, music, and paintings great themes and great characters from the Book of Mormon.

I have a vision of thousands of missionaries going into the mission field with hundreds of passages memorized from the Book of Mormon so that they might feed the needs of a spiritually famished world.

I have a vision of the whole Church getting nearer to God by abiding by the precepts of the Book of Mormon.

Indeed, I have a vision of flooding the earth with the Book of Mormon. (Ezra Taft Benson, "Flooding the Earth with the Book of Mormon," *Ensign*, Nov. 1988, 4.)

President Gordon B. Hinckley declared:

Those who have read [the Book of Mormon] prayerfully, be they rich or poor, learned or unlearned, have grown under its power. . .

Without reservation I promise you that if you will prayerfully read the Book of Mormon, regardless of how many times you previously have read it, there will come into your hearts . . . the Spirit of the Lord. There will come a strengthened resolution to walk in obedience to his commandments, and there will come a stronger testimony of the living reality of the Son of God. (Gordon B. Hinckley, "The Power of the Book of Mormon," *Ensign*, June 1988.)

Elder M. Russell Ballard has reminded us:

The Book of Mormon, above all other books that I know of, is the greatest source we have for answers to real-life problems. . .

How many times peace has come into the lives of those who are struggling with real problems when they read the Book of Mormon! The examples of spiritual guidance that emanate from the book are without number. (M. Russell Ballard, "We Add Our Witness," *Tambuli*, Dec. 1989.)

This book contains forty-four questions that have often been asked about the uncertainties of life. The questions will be stated at the start of each section. A scripture will then be used to answer the question and be shown on the left side of the page. Insight and commentary will be included on the right side of the page. It should be remembered that there are many more answers to each of the questions found within the pages of the Book of Mormon. This is neither a prescriptive set of solutions to each stated question nor an exhaustive collection of remedies to every question or problem we might encounter. The book is meant to help the reader understand the principle that The Book of Mormon, which was compiled from a library of plates and records by prophets who saw and understood our day, also gives us answers to the challenges and questions that would pester and disturb our souls today.

You might want to take a traditional approach and read this book cover-to-cover. Another way to approach it is to read it by scanning through and selecting a few questions at a time, thereby executing your own study while adding additional answers. A few blank pages have been included at the end of the book for your personal questions or those asked by your friends or investigators. Perhaps you will discover that the format of this book will provide one of its most important take-aways. It is a way to study scripture. Identify a question, and then proceed to search the word of God through His holy prophets to find applicable answers for you and for those you teach.

Enjoy the process of finding answers—not only those few that are included by the author, but also those that you find on your own through the guidance of the Spirit in Church classes, or in discussion with family and friends. The very best answers might, in fact, be those you find within the pages of the "greatest handbook for living"—the Book of Mormon.

QUESTION 1

How can I find guidance and direction in my life?

Answer: **2 Nephi 32:3, 8–9**	Commentary:
3 Angels speak by the power of the Holy Ghost; wherefore, they speak the words of Christ. Wherefore, I said unto you, feast upon the words of Christ; for behold, the words of Christ will tell you all things what ye should do.	*Connecting with Father in Heaven—who loves us—through prayer is one of the most important principles to learn when we are seeking to find guidance and direction for our lives.*
8 And now, my beloved brethren, I perceive that ye ponder still in your hearts; and it grieveth me that I must speak concerning this thing. For if ye would hearken unto the Spirit which teacheth a man to pray, ye would know that ye must pray; for the evil spirit teacheth not a man to pray, but teacheth him that he must not pray.	*Someone once said, "If you want to talk to God, then pray. If you want God to talk to you, read the scriptures." Casual, occasional chats with Heavenly Father and quick skimming through holy writ will not likely open up the channels of heaven to help us find His will and guidance for our lives. Nor will passive action on our part invite assertive influence from Him.*
	Because prayer, coupled with scripture study, is so important, Nephi warns us

that the adversary, Satan, will do everything possible to "teach us" not to establish a connection with Heavenly Father in prayer. By doing so, scriptures will be less instructive, if at all.

9 But behold, I say unto you that ye must pray always, and not faint; that ye must not perform any thing unto the Lord save in the first place ye shall pray unto the Father in the name of Christ, that he will consecrate thy performance unto thee, that thy performance may be for the welfare of thy soul.

The Lord promises us that if we pray with real intent and seek His will by reading His words in the scriptures, then He will "consecrate" (or make holy) our efforts for the well being of our souls.

Not everything we do will go as we plan. However, as we seek His guidance through prayer and through reading His word—what we do with faith in the Lord will ultimately be turned for our good. Centering our trust on Him is fundamental to receiving the guidance He desires to give us.

Answer: 1 Nephi 19:23

23 And I did read many things unto them which were written in the books of Moses; but that I might more fully persuade them to believe in the Lord their Redeemer I did read unto them that which was written by the prophet Isaiah; for I did liken all scriptures unto us, that it might be for our profit and learning.

Commentary:

Nephi recognized the role of Jesus Christ as Savior and Redeemer of the world. He knew that Isaiah was truly a prophet who taught the nature and mission of Jesus Christ at every opportunity.

He knew that true and influential guidance and direction in the lives of all Heavenly Father's children would include the Savior and that He must be the "hub," the "nucleus," or the "heart" of our lives—from where we are now to what we become in the end. In order to accomplish that, Nephi "did liken all scriptures unto us."

Remember, if we want to talk to Heavenly Father, we pray. If we want Heavenly Father to talk to us, we read the scriptures. Therefore, scripture can speak to us and provide us with the moral compass to properly orient us.

So, whatever guidance and direction we seek must be centered on Jesus Christ and His will. We must forever ask, "What did Christ do in His every circumstance to find the guidance and direction He needed—not only in His most challenging moments, but also in His day-to-day journeys?"

As we seek guidance and direction in our lives, we look for how Christ traveled life's thorny path. We look for patterns in the lives of those who followed Him, and we "liken" their responses, reactions, and eventual choices that led them to the Savior to our situations. We can also learn from outcomes in the lives of those who were not so centered on Him and allowed themselves to wander in strange roads.

Answer: **1 Nephi 16**
(the entire chapter with emphasis on verses 26–30)

26 And it came to pass that the voice of the Lord said unto him: Look upon the ball, and behold the things which are written.

Commentary:

If there was ever time when Nephi needed guidance and direction, it was in a moment when everything had gone awry for him and his family. Their bows had either broken or lost their spring; they seemed doomed to starvation and eventual death. Everyone, including Lehi, was murmuring and second guessing their journey to the

27 And it came to pass that when my father beheld the things which were written upon the ball, he did fear and tremble exceedingly, and also my brethren and the sons of Ishmael and our wives.

28 And it came to pass that I, Nephi, beheld the pointers which were in the ball, that they did work according to the faith and diligence and heed which we did give unto them.

29 And there was also written upon them a new writing, which was plain to be read, which did give us understanding concerning the ways of the Lord; and it was written and changed from time to time, according to the faith and diligence which we gave unto it. And thus we see that by small means the Lord can bring about great things.

30 And it came to pass that I, Nephi, did go forth up into the top of the mountain, according to the directions which were given upon the ball.

wilderness. They needed guidance and direction.

The Lord knew that they would need help to get through the tough experiences, so He had already provided them with a way to receive guidance and direction in puzzling times—the Liahona. A tangible instrument. Something specific they could look to for answers in their times of need.

There was one major catch. The God-given instrument worked "according to the faith and diligence and heed which we gave" unto the pointers. Finding answers, true guidance, and direction comes with a price. We must give heed with faith and a lot of diligence to the instruments God has already given us. The scriptures, priesthood leaders, prophets, written blessings, general conference addresses, temple attendance, and—most of all—the nudgings and stirrings of the Holy Ghost will give us understanding and will be altered "from time to time, according to the faith and diligence" we give to them.

Nephi reminds us many times that by "small means" the Lord brings about "great things." Much of the time, we already have the guidance and direction we need. We just need to access those seemingly small means by giving "heed" and exercising faith and diligence in Christ.

Answer: **Alma 37:35–47**

35 O, remember, my son, and learn wisdom in thy youth; yea, learn in thy youth to keep the commandments of God.

36 Yea, and cry unto God for all thy support; yea, let all thy doings be unto the Lord, and whithersoever thou goest let it be in the Lord; yea, let all thy thoughts be directed unto the Lord; yea, let the affections of thy heart be placed upon the Lord forever.

37 Counsel with the Lord in all thy doings, and he will direct thee for good; yea, when thou liest down at night lie down unto the Lord, that he may watch over you in your sleep; and when thou risest in the morning let thy heart be full of thanks unto God; and if ye do these things, ye shall be lifted up at the last day.

38 And now, my son, I have somewhat to say concerning the thing which our fathers call a ball, or director—or our fathers called it Liahona, which is, being interpreted, a compass; and the Lord prepared it.

39 And behold, there cannot any man work after the manner of so curious a workmanship. And

Commentary:

There are many answers in this block of scripture that question of finding guidance and direction in our lives. It all begins with remembering that if we really do want help from Heavenly Father, then we have to do things His way.

Certainly we pray. We seek to know what we should do in every situation. Alma's counsel to his extraordinary son Helaman was to remember that prayer is not only an act which we "do" a time or two each day; prayer is a lifestyle! It is a constant petition to help us in our wonderings as well as our wanderings. We should be in constant pursuit of doing things the Lord's way, which is identified in His commandments and teachings. In our hearts we appeal to Him for the capacity to see things more clearly. As we search and see more clearly, we commit that our doings will be in His way.

Alma reminds Helaman about that ball, or director—the Liahona. He invites his son to remember that the ball given to his grandfather, Lehi, was more than just man's workmanship. It was a compass. If we want to know which way is North and which way is South in order to orient ourselves to where we are and which way we should go, we consult a compass, which gives us our bearings. Then he says simply, "The Lord prepared it." He seems to tell Alma as well as us, "You must know that Heavenly Father cares

behold, it was prepared to show unto our fathers the course which they should travel in the wilderness.

about which direction you go in your life. He cares enough that he gives you a way to seek and find guidance. If you want to know which course you should travel—which direction, when, and how—then you must also recognize that Heavenly Father loves you and wants to help you in your desire. He has given you a way. He will direct you.

40 And it did work for them according to their faith in God; therefore, if they had faith to believe that God could cause that those spindles should point the way they should go, behold, it was done; therefore they had this miracle, and also many other miracles wrought by the power of God, day by day.

It did work "according to their faith." Now we get to the real operating system of finding guidance for the questions in our lives. When things seem a little fuzzy to us, it's time to move our feet with faith in the Lord Jesus Christ! Faith is an action word! Faith is a principle of action and of power. Faith always moves its possessor to action and carries an assurance of the fulfillment of those things we hope for. To receive the guidance and direction in life that we seek and to experience the miracle of receiving it, we must do the small and simple actions that demonstrate our faith in Christ.

41 Nevertheless, because those miracles were worked by small means it did show unto them marvelous works. They were slothful, and forgot to exercise their faith and diligence and then those marvelous works ceased, and they did not progress in their journey;

Lehi's family had the direction—the compass. But when they became sluggish and casual in their faith (action) in the Lord, then revelation regarding their future course halted. When their guidance system ceased, they did not progress in their journey.

42 Therefore, they tarried in the wilderness, or did not travel a

They meandered and wandered instead of moving on a straight course as they once had. As they zigzagged through

direct course, and were afflicted hunger and thirst, because of their transgressions.

the wilderness, they were afflicted with hunger and thirst because of their lack of righteous focus. Things did not go as they had cognitively determined, and instead of finding life well defined, they struggled. The Lord's way of giving guidance was stayed because they strayed in their faith and trust in God and His Son Jesus Christ.

43 And now, my son, I would that ye should understand that these things are not without a shadow; for as our fathers were slothful to give heed to this compass (now these things were temporal) they did not prosper; even so it is with things which are spiritual.

We are reminded in this "type and shadow" that sustained prosperity and progression in our lives comes as we heed the Lord's guidance and direction, which generally comes through His word.

44 For behold, it is as easy to give heed to the word of Christ, which will point to you a straight course to eternal bliss, as it was for our fathers to give heed to this compass, which would point unto them a straight course to the promised land.

To "give heed" means "to take note, to listen to, to mark, to consider, to follow, to obey, to abide by, or to be alert to something." The antonym is "to disregard." Guidance and direction comes to those who pay attention to His word and move their feet in action toward worthy goals and ambitions. It is really not any harder than that. As we seek guidance and direction, we actively seek to understand his word. We avoid becoming lethargic and casual in the easiness of the way as the "guidance system" is working well. If we falter, the director loses its effectiveness and often stops providing guidance altogether.

45 And now I say, is there not a type in this thing? For just as surely as this director did bring our fathers, by following its course, to the promised land, shall the words of Christ, if we follow their course, carry us beyond this vale of sorrow into a far better land of promise.

46 O my son, do not let us be slothful because of the easiness of the way; for so was it with our fathers; for so was it prepared for them, that if they would look they might live;

Helaman is admonished to be attentive to the "system," to keep it in working order, and to look to God and live. Remember Him and keep His commandments in faith that he will "guide us."

even so it is with us. The way is prepared, and if we will look we may live forever. 47 And now, my son, see that ye take care of these sacred things, yea, see that ye look to God and live. Go unto this people and declare the word, and be sober. My son, farewell.	*Our moment of truth lies in our "action" when we have complete trust that our feet are moving according to His will—and that He will move us to course correction if we get a little off.*

Answer: **Alma 56:47–48**	Commentary:
47 Now they never had fought, yet they did not fear death; and they did think more upon the liberty of their fathers than they did upon their lives; yea, they had been taught by their mothers, that if they did not doubt, God would deliver them. 48 And they rehearsed unto me the words of their mothers, saying: We do not doubt our mothers knew it.	*The 2,060 young men known as the stripling warriors had grown to have complete trust in their mothers, who had done so much to teach them to have faith in their Lord, Jesus Christ.* *During their biggest moments of decision and questions regarding who they were and how they would react to the invitation to participate in the war, they relied upon a memory of those who had taught them in their younger years. This provides a pattern that can help us. When we are wondering what we should do and the direction in which we should go, we can stop and ask, "What did parents, priesthood leaders, and teachers already teach us regarding the question or dilemma we are facing?" Oftentimes remembering is sufficient to stir up recollections of past guidance and wisdom.*

Answer: **Ether 12:6**	Commentary:
6 And now, I, Moroni, would speak somewhat concerning these things; I would show unto the world that faith is things which are hoped for and not seen; wherefore, dispute not because ye see not, for ye receive no witness until after the trial of your faith.	*Sometimes when we seek guidance and direction in our lives, a loving Heavenly Father may withhold immediate answers or clarity to our dilemma. He knows that the development of our faith in His Son is far more important than immediate enlightenment. Perhaps we must continue to increase our faith and exhibit our trust in Him, to the end that our faith is no longer on trial. But rather, it is unshakable in knowing that we really do know that He is mindful of our course; we really do desire His will and not our own. The trial of our faith is a true and important principle to always remember.*

Answer: **Alma 5:46**	Commentary:
46 Behold, I say unto you they are made known unto me by the Holy Spirit of God. Behold, I have fasted and prayed many days that I might know these things of myself. And now I do know of myself that they are true; for the Lord God hath made them manifest unto me by his Holy Spirit; and this is the spirit of revelation which is in me.	*Sometimes our quest for guidance and direction must include "many days" of fasting and prayers, and not just a little meditation and reading of scripture. The Lord is interested in giving us answers to our questions and perplexities. We must recognize as well that He understands that our growth and development is paramount. We must also know that His will and His way will eventually manifest or be revealed through the channel of the Holy Ghost.*

Answer: **Moroni 10:3–5**	Commentary:
3 Behold, I would exhort you that when ye shall read these things, if it be wisdom in God that ye should read them, that ye would remember how merciful the Lord hath been unto the children of men, from the creation of Adam even down until the time that ye shall receive these things, and ponder it in your hearts.	*Heavenly Father really is merciful to His children, and He wants them to grow and become like Him. He therefore invites us to engage in a divine process of pondering and praying with sincerity and real intent in the name of His Son Jesus Christ.*
4 And when ye shall receive these things, I would exhort you that ye would ask God, the Eternal Father, in the name of Christ, if these things are not true; and if ye shall ask with a sincere heart, with real intent, having faith in Christ, he will manifest the truth of it unto you, by the power of the Holy Ghost.	*It would be well that after we have prayed and pondered, we come with a proposed answer to the guidance and direction we are seeking. It is as if we say, "Father, I've pondered, prayed, and acted in faith in thy Son, and here is my conclusion. Now, Father, let me ask thee: Is this acceptable to thee?"*
5 And by the power of the Holy Ghost ye may know the truth of all things	*The Lord promises He will answer via the power of the real teacher and guide, the Holy Ghost.*

QUESTION 2

How do I know if I am feeling the Spirit?

Answer: Mosiah 4:3

3 And it came to pass that after they had spoken these words the Spirit of the Lord came upon them, and they were filled with joy, having received a remission of their sins, and having peace of conscience, because of the exceeding faith which they had in Jesus Christ who should come, according to the words which king Benjamin had spoken unto them.

Commentary:

King Benjamin gave his classic sermon from a tower near the temple to a multitude of followers. Believing in the words of King Benjamin gave them the gift of feeling the Spirit. That feeling is described as joy (described in the dictionary as "gladness, rejoicing, delight, pleasure, elation, enjoyment, and exhilaration"). Feeling the Spirit is also described as understanding that we are acceptable to our Heavenly Father—having peace of conscience. The dictionary defines peace as "tranquility, calmness, and quiet restfulness." The Middle English origin of the word mean "inner thoughts or knowledge." Knowi whether or not we feel the Spirit then something to do with peace and calm in our inner thoughts. The Spirit inspires an attitude of quiet assurance that we are on the right track or that our actions are approved by Heavenly Father, who desires the best for us. As always, it comes to us based on our faith in Jesus Christ.

Answer: **Alma 32:28**

28 Now, we will compare the word unto a seed. Now, if ye give place, that a seed may be planted in your heart, behold, if it be a true seed, or a good seed, if ye do not cast it out by your unbelief, that ye will resist the Spirit of the Lord, behold, it will begin to swell within your breasts; and when you feel these swelling motions, ye will begin to say within yourselves—It must needs be that this is a good seed, or that the word is good, for it beginneth to enlarge my soul; yea, it beginneth to enlighten my understanding, yea, it beginneth to be delicious to me.

Commentary:

The metaphor of the seed is a good one for us as we seek to know whether or not we are feeling the spirit. When we "act in faith" in the Lord and plant good seeds, we will feel enlightened and enlarged, and we are able to see things more clearly.

Our choices, instead of being clouded by doubt or indecision, will yield certain delightful or pleasurable feelings. Alma calls it "delicious." It is interesting that he indicates it "beginneth" to be pleasurable or heavenly. He doesn't say that it happens all at once. Impressions and swelling motions are often gradual—line upon line. Enlightening happens gently or bit by bit.

Answer: **Moroni 7:44–47**

44 If so, his faith and hope is vain, for none is acceptable before God, save the meek and lowly in heart; and if a man be meek and lowly in heart, and confesses by the power of the Holy Ghost that Jesus is the Christ, he must needs have charity; for if he have not charity he is

Commentary:

When we have the Spirit of the Holy Ghost with us, we have love for everyone. When we don't have the Spirit, we are irritable, unkind, and self-centered.

That's one way we can know if we are feeling the influence of the Spirit in our lives.

nothing; wherefore he must needs have charity.	*Our "love gauge" is particularly high.*
45 And charity suffereth long, and is kind, and envieth not, and is not puffed up, seeketh not her own, is not easily provoked, thinketh no evil, and rejoiceth not in iniquity but rejoiceth in the truth, beareth all things, believeth all things, hopeth all things, endureth all things.	*Love is a feeling. When we have the Spirit, we feel warmth of character. We feel more kind. We are concerned about others. We feel like participating in activities that are good. We are not inclined toward doubt. We are not prone to be irritated with others or their actions. We are unselfish. We feel inclined toward being friendly. We have a general feeling of goodwill.*
46 Wherefore, my beloved brethren, if ye have not charity, ye are nothing, for charity never faileth. Wherefore, cleave unto charity, which is the greatest of all, for all things must fail—	*"Love" is also a verb.*
47 But charity is the pure love of Christ, and it endureth forever; and whoso is found possessed of it at the last day, it shall be well with him.	*When we have the Spirit, we care more, adore more, and show more pleasure in good things. We smile and look beyond ourselves. We do more lovable things. We act with love in a spirit of love.*

Answer: **Helaman 5:44–48**	Commentary:
44 And Nephi and Lehi were in the midst of them; yea, they were encircled about; yea, they were as if in the midst of a flaming fire, yet it did harm them not, neither did it take hold upon the walls of the prison; and they were filled with that joy which is unspeakable and full of glory.	*When we feel the Spirit, we feel joy. The meaning of "joy" is "delight, great pleasure, gladness, happiness, and rejoicing," to name a few.* *It's described in this verse as "unspeakable and full of glory." That can be an evidence of "feeling the Spirit."*

45 And behold, the Holy Spirit of God did come down from heaven, and did enter into their hearts, and they were filled as if with fire, and they could speak forth marvelous words.	*When we feel the Spirit, it comes both to and from the heart. When we know something, it comes both from the mind and from the heart.*
46 And it came to pass that there came a voice unto them, yea, a pleasant voice, as if it were a whisper, saying:	*The voice of the Spirit is pleasant to our minds, and most often is quiet as a whisper. It is always accompanied by a feeling of peace.*
47 Peace, peace be unto you, because of your faith in my Well Beloved, who was from the foundation of the world.	
48 And now, when they heard this they cast up their eyes as if to behold from whence the voice came; and behold, they saw the heavens open; and angels came down out of heaven and ministered unto them.	

Answer: **Helaman 5:29–30**	Commentary:
29 And it came to pass that there came a voice as if it were above the cloud of darkness, saying: Repent ye, repent ye, and seek no more to destroy my servants whom I have sent unto you to declare good tidings.	*There are a couple of things to note in these verses:* *First, the very first thing the "voice" from heaven states is an invitation to repent. When we feel the Spirit, while we don't feel an overpowering sense of guilt, we do feel a sweet heartfelt desire to repent—to change—and to be a better person. We can all become better. Repentance there-*
30 And it came to pass when they heard this voice, and beheld that it was not a voice of thunder, neither	*fore becomes a lifestyle rather than an*

was it a voice of a great tumultuous noise, but behold, it was a still voice of perfect mildness, as if it had been a whisper, and it did pierce even to the very soul—

event. The lifelong feeling to repent (and put ourselves a step up in our actions) is a gift of feeling the Spirit.

Second, the Spirit is quiet. "Stillness" and "mildness" are words often used to describe how one feels when they experience the Spirit. It might be a whisper, but it stirs the soul and penetrates the heart.

QUESTION 3
Why do bad things happen to good people?

Answer: **1 Nephi 11:17**

17 And I said unto him: I know that he loveth his children; nevertheless, I do not know the meaning of all things.

Also see **Alma 40:3−5**

3 Behold, he bringeth to pass the resurrection of the dead. But behold, my son, the resurrection is not yet. Now, I unfold unto you a mystery; nevertheless, there are many mysteries which are kept, that no one knoweth them save

Commentary:

The answer to some questions ultimately has to be reduced to this response. We have to cease speculation in favor of interpretation of what we do know. We know we have a Heavenly Father who loves us. His primary objective in His plan is that we grow and learn in this laboratory of life—complete with thorns, thistles, and noxious weeds. Sometimes that knowledge must be enough.

Sometimes we just don't have enough information or understanding. Our view from our earthly perspective is incomplete. We have to rely on our knowledge that He does love us and that all experience will be consecrated for our development and learning.

God himself. But I show unto you one thing which I have inquired diligently of God that I might know —that is concerning the resurrection.

4 Behold, there is a time appointed that all shall come forth from the dead. Now when this time cometh no one knows; but God knoweth the time which is appointed.

5 Now, whether there shall be one time, or a second time, or a third time, that men shall come forth from the dead, it mattereth not; for God knoweth all these things; and it sufficeth me to know that this is the case—that there is a time appointed that all shall rise from the dead.

In Alma 40, Alma is speaking to his son Corianton, who has had a significant challenge with immorality. In this chapter, however, he states that Corianton is flirting with another challenge—an unbridled desire to know the mysteries. Corianton is questioning something that has not happened yet and won't for almost another century—the resurrection. He questions, "How does someone come back to life, and who decides who gets to be first?" Likened to us, the question could be, "Why do bad things happen to good people?"

Alma simply says, "I don't know. No one knows. Whether there's going to be a first resurrection, a second, a third, or a twenty-ninth, I don't know. What I do know is that God knows all these things. Knowing that He knows is good enough. He will take care of those details, and I am simply happy that there will be a resurrection of the dead and that I can participate and receive the blessing of it. That's good enough for me." May it be so with all of us. Know that He knows, and trust that He loves us. All will be managed in His omniscient hands.

Answer: **Mosiah 23:21–22**

Commentary:

21 Nevertheless the Lord seeth fit to chasten his people; yea, he trieth their patience and their faith.

God's purpose is to help us learn to be like Him. To be "chaste" means to be "pure." To be pure, we must be purified. Chastening is to purify and make clean. Good people become better and have a greater capacity to trust Heavenly Father.

22 Nevertheless—whosoever putteth his trust in him the same shall be lifted up at the last day. Yea, and thus it was with this people.	*If we know Heavenly Father loves us, then we understand "bad things" are allowed to happen so that His children can be purified and cleansed. We learn patience and trust. Our faith can increase when we experience or observe challenges we don't understand. We are forced to ask a fundamental question: "Does Heavenly Father love of all His children, and do I trust Him?"*

Answer: **Helaman 12:3**	Commentary:
3 And thus we see that except the Lord doth chasten his people with many afflictions, yea, except he doth visit them with death and with terror, and with famine and with all manner of pestilence, they will not remember him.	*When we are shaken up, we tend to become more focused on spiritual things. We remember the Plan of Happiness, and we are brought to a "remembrance" of who God and Christ are.*

All of us are children of our Heavenly Father. He has a singular objective: to bring to pass the immortality and eternal lives of all of us, His children. He wants His children to become like Him and to have what He has. To take us from mortal infants and help us to become like Him, we must experience many things. From the fall of Adam and Eve to the present, He has stated that "cursed shall be the ground for thy sake." The word "sake" means "benefit, advantage, good, well-being, welfare, interest, or profit." In other words, God said that "life will be very different now, but it is for your sake, benefit, advantage, good, well-being, welfare, interest, and profit." Chastening or making pure is a long, hard process. Good people are not exempt. |

QUESTION 4

How can I cheerfully accept my tribulations and suffering?

Answer: **2 Nephi 2:1–2**	Commentary:
1 And now, Jacob, I speak unto you: Thou art my first-born in the days of my tribulation in the wilderness. And behold, in thy childhood thou hast suffered afflictions and much sorrow, because of the rudeness of thy brethren.	*This is a wonderful scripture! It explains so much about how afflictions and suffering are actually used by the Lord to bless us.*
2 Nevertheless, Jacob, my first-born in the wilderness, thou knowest the greatness of God; and he shall consecrate thine afflictions for thy gain.	*Jacob was the first child born to Lehi and Sariah while they were en route to Bountiful, or Irreantum, the place of many waters (where they would finally build the ship and leave for the Promised Land). Everything Jacob had known from his birth to approximately age eight was "affliction" of every kind. The lack of food and nourishment was hard, but the emotional mistreatment and rudeness of older brothers must have been worse.*

Lehi teaches us a really important scripture when he states to his son Jacob, "You know the greatness of God." Understanding the omniscience of an all-knowing God the Father helps us know why we have afflictions, sorrow, troubles, or seeming misfortune. Once we know and remember that great truth, then Lehi's next great teaching helps us answer the vexing question of the soul, "How can I cheerfully accept tribulation and suffering?" Lehi promises his son—and each one of us who encounters hard days, experiences a large dose of misery, or finds that the wretchedness of life is too often on our side of the street— that God our Father, who knows all, "shall consecrate" our afflictions for our gain. That is enough to make our "hard days" worth it! To "consecrate" means "to make holy, to bless, to make sacred, to devote, or to make hallow." When we know that our heartbreaks, stresses, and woes have purpose, it's easier to take them in stride with a smile instead of a scowl. Perhaps we don't have to glory in our trials, but we can cheerfully make it through them.

Answer: **2 Nephi 2:11**

11 For it must needs be, that there is an opposition in all things. If not so, my first-born in the wilderness, righteousness could not be brought to pass, neither wickedness, neither holiness nor misery, neither good nor bad. Wherefore, all things must

Commentary:

Perhaps one of the best ways—and certainly one of the first, important steps—in cheerfully accepting trials and suffering is to accept the great truth that opposition is a part of earthly life. When a baby is born and takes its first breath, that baby

needs be a compound in one; wherefore, if it should be one body it must needs remain as dead, having no life neither death, nor corruption nor incorruption, happiness nor misery, neither sense nor insensibility.

is introduced to the need for air to live. We breath in and out somewhere between 16,000 times per day on the average, or nearly 6 million times per year. If we stop breathing, we die!

We never argue about the purpose of oxygen to breathe. It is a part of life! And so is opposition. As long as we live in this world, there will always be opposition. Accepting that important truth helps us accept opposition without wondering why or when it will stop. We can then focus on learning from it and perhaps grow a sense of gratitude and glory. It's a part of life. There is purpose in it!

Answer: **Alma 7:11–12**

Commentary:

11 And he shall go forth, suffering pains and afflictions and temptations of every kind; and this that the word might be fulfilled which saith he will take upon him the pains and the sicknesses of his people.

12 And he will take upon him death, that he may loose the bands of death which bind his people; and he will take upon him their infirmities, that his bowels may be filled with mercy, according to the flesh, that he may know according to the flesh how to succor his people according to their infirmities.

As Alma preaches to the people of Gideon, he prophesies of Christ who will come to suffer not only for our sins, but also for our pains, afflictions, and temptations of every kind. He has experienced "our pains" and felt "our afflictions." He did this because of His love for us. When we come upon wretched hardships and distressful sorrows, remembering that He has suffered exactly those afflictions (along with the afflictions of every other human being that's ever lived or will live on this earth) can help us appreciate His love for us.

Remembering His love helps us to be a little more accepting of our tribulations.

Answer: **Alma 26:27–31**	Commentary:
27 Now when our hearts were depressed, and we were about to turn back, behold, the Lord comforted us, and said: Go amongst thy brethren, the Lamanites, and bear with patience thine afflictions, and I will give unto you success.	*Ammon is talking to his brothers and friends after they have returned from their mission to the Lamanites. And he reminds them how they felt at the beginning: they were about to turn back and go home. However, he rehearses, it was the Lord who comforted them, admonished them to "go and to bear with patience" the challenges they would experience, and even promised them great success.*
28 And now behold, we have come, and been forth amongst them; and we have been patient in our sufferings, and we have suffered every privation; yea, we have traveled from house to house, relying upon the mercies of the world—not upon the mercies of the world alone but upon the mercies of God.	*Ammon evokes more memories on the foundation of where they had been and how they had felt at the beginning of their fourteen-year mission. He says, "We were patient, we did suffer, we were mocked, people even spit on us and slapped our faces. We were imprisoned and bound with ropes and had stones thrown at us."*
29 And we have entered into their houses and taught them, and we have taught them in their streets; yea, and we have taught them upon their hills; and we have also entered into their temples and their synagogues and taught them; and we have been cast out, and mocked, and spit upon, and smote upon our cheeks; and we have been stoned, and taken and bound with strong cords, and cast into prison; and through the power and wisdom of God we have been delivered again.	*However, never forget that through God's power and wisdom, they were delivered from their challenges. Heavenly Father did not forget them! They had a mission to fulfill, and His promise was that if they continued in those moments of tribulation and suffering, they would be blessed to save souls.*

30 And we have suffered all manner of afflictions, and all this, that perhaps we might be the means of saving some soul; and we supposed that our joy would be full if perhaps we could be the means of saving some.

31 Now behold, we can look forth and see the fruits of our labors; and are they few? I say unto you, Nay, they are many; yea, and we can witness of their sincerity, because of their love towards their brethren and also towards us.

Finally, Ammon reminds them that the fruits of their labors and their reward for continuing on through those hard and difficult experiences were unbelievably grand! Tens of thousands of people were blessed by their message. The results of their bearing their afflictions were significant. The results were made even sweeter by the love and sincerity of their converts.

Remember, Heavenly Father will reward and bless those who suffer and sacrifice for Him.

QUESTION 5

Why do we have agency, and
what is its purpose in the big picture?

Answer: **2 Nephi 2:26–30**	Commentary:
26 And the Messiah cometh in the fulness of time, that he may redeem the children of men from the fall. And because that they are redeemed from the fall they have become free forever, knowing good from evil; to act for themselves and not to be acted upon, save it be by the punishment of the law at the great and last day, according to the commandments which God hath given.	*Agency is at the foundation of the Great Plan of Happiness. The Plan of Salvation wouldn't exist if there were no agency.* *From the beginning, we have been free to choose. Because of the Light of Christ that is in every person on earth, we can know what is good and what is evil. We are free to act for ourselves and choose.*
27 Wherefore, men are free according to the flesh; and all things are given them which are expedient unto man. And they are free to choose liberty and eternal life, through the great Mediator of all	*We choose liberty and eternal life through the Mediator Jesus Christ, or we choose captivity and death through the devil, who has one singular objective—to spoil all that is good, that we might become miserable as he is.*

men, or to choose captivity and death, according to the captivity and power of the devil; for he seeketh that all men might be miserable like unto himself.

28 And now, my sons, I would that ye should look to the great Mediator, and hearken unto his great commandments; and be faithful unto his words, and choose eternal life, according to the will of his Holy Spirit

Given agency, or choice, we simply choose our path. Choosing and looking to Christ in our quest for happiness brings us just that—happiness.

29 And not choose eternal death, according to the will of the flesh and the evil which is therein, which giveth the spirit of the devil power to captivate, to bring you down to hell, that he may reign over you in his own kingdom.

Choosing evil will captivate us and ultimately bring us unhappiness and misery.

30 I have spoken these few words unto you all, my sons, in the last days of my probation; and I have chosen the good part, according to the words of the prophet. And I have none other object save it be the everlasting welfare of your souls. Amen.

Answer: **Alma 12:31**

Commentary:

31 Wherefore, he gave commandments unto men, they having first transgressed the first commandments as to things which were temporal, and becoming as Gods, knowing good from evil, placing

Heavenly Father's Plan of Happiness—our road to Salvation—requires that we, His children, have the opportunity to make our own choices. We are placed in earthly situations and circumstances that test our ability to exercise the

themselves in a state to act, or being placed in a state to according to their wills and pleasures, whether to do evil or to do good—

power He has given to us to choose, according to our own will and pleasure, whether or not we will choose Him and His ways.

Notice the word "pleasures." The word means "happiness, delight, joy, gladness, satisfaction, or enjoyment"—to name a few. In other words, we are here on earth to school our attitude and to find enjoyment in doing those things that God has commanded us. Agency then, in the big picture, gives us an opportunity to train and teach ourselves through discipline to be disciples while finding pleasure in so doing. ("Discipline" is the root word of "disciple.")

Answer: **Helaman 14:30–31**

30 And now remember, remember, my brethren, that whosoever perisheth, perisheth unto himself; and whosoever doeth iniquity, doeth it unto himself; for behold, ye are free; ye are permitted to act for yourselves; for behold, God hath given unto you a knowledge and he hath made you free.

31 He hath given unto you that ye might know good from evil, and he hath given unto you that ye might choose life or death; and ye can do good and be restored unto that which is good, or have that which is good restored unto you; or ye can

Commentary:

Agency is a fundamental principle in the plan. We choose for ourselves to bring emotional, spiritual, and temporal challenges for happiness here and through the eternities.

Simply stated, Heavenly Father has given us—through the light of Christ, which is given to every man—the knowledge sufficient to know good from evil. All must have the power to choose one over the other.

Mormon also teaches that in the matter of agency, "What goes around, comes around," or "What you plant is that which you reap." As we make good choices (plant

do evil, and have that which is evil restored unto you.	*good seeds), we can expect positive results (a good harvest). Agency simply gives us the power to plant seeds and then expect that action to be "restored" or given back to us in a positive harvest.*

Answer: **2 Nephi 10:23**	Commentary:
23 Therefore, cheer up your hearts, and remember that ye are free to act for yourselves—to choose the way of everlasting death or the way of eternal life.	*Nephi is quick to remind us that it is a very happy matter that we are free! Agency is a gift from a loving Father to His children—a gift to be able to choose and to act for themselves.* *We must remember that in the "big picture," agency is something to rejoice and take great pleasure in. "Cheer up . . . and remember," he reminds us.*

QUESTION 6
How can I improve my marriage?

Answer: 1 Nephi 5:1–9

1 And it came to pass that after we had come down into the wilderness unto our father, behold, he was filled with joy, and also my mother, Sariah, was exceedingly glad, for she truly had mourned because of us.

2 For she had supposed that we had perished in the wilderness; and she also had complained against my father, telling him that he was a visionary man; saying: Behold thou hast led us forth from the land of our inheritance, and my sons are no more, and we perish in the wilderness.

Commentary:

This is one of those stories in the Book of Mormon that invites us to see the process of what happens when there is controversy and discord in a marriage relationship.

Sariah had followed Lehi's lead in leaving their home, possessions, friends, acquaintances, and all that comes with the comforts of home in Jerusalem.

When Lehi sent his sons back to Jerusalem (a distance of just under 200 miles) she might have wondered about the wisdom of that request. When the boys hadn't returned in what she considered to be more-than-adequate time, Sariah expressed her doubts. It might have been one of those "I told you so" moments in a marriage. Or

3 And after this manner of language had my mother complained against my father.

4 And it had come to pass that my father spake unto her, saying: I know that I am a visionary man; for if I had not seen the things of God in a vision I should not have known the goodness of God, but had tarried at Jerusalem, and had perished with my brethren.

5 But behold, I have obtained a land of promise, in the which things I do rejoice; yea, and I know that the Lord will deliver my sons out of the hands of Laban, and bring them down again unto us in the wilderness.

6 And after this manner of language did my father, Lehi, comfort my mother, Sariah, concerning us, while we journeyed in the wilderness up to the land of Jerusalem, to obtain the record of the Jews.

7 And when we had returned to the tent of my father, behold their joy was full, and my mother was comforted.

perhaps Sariah felt she really had been supportive in every way; but finally, with the apparent loss of her sons, it was the last straw. She unleashed pent-up feelings and accused Lehi of being a dreamer or fantasist—a wishful thinker.

Lehi acknowledged that visions had impacted their lives and understandings. He reminded her that the price they were paying with their challenges was designed to get them safely to a better place. Knowing that the vision came from the Lord, he assured her that their sons were not dead, but would return to them.

He sought to give her comfort and expressed trust in the Lord in the matter. He could have lashed back at her, pointing out her whining or her nagging. He could have walked away and stonewalled. He might have accused her of being high maintenance or of losing her faith in God. She, on the other hand, could have retorted to his encouraging optimism in anger. She could have drawn a proverbial line in the sand and said, "this is where I get off." Instead, they apparently listened and discussed. She sensed his desire to do as he was commanded. In the end she was "comforted," realizing that they were in this together and with the Lord. Ultimately we see—as she sees—how her attitude can impact the marriage. Lehi apparently is empathetic and tries to see things from her perspective and point of view.

8 And she spake, saying: Now I know of a surety that the Lord hath commanded my husband to flee into the wilderness; yea, and I also know of a surety that the Lord hath protected my sons, and delivered them out of the hands of Laban, and given them power whereby they could accomplish the thing which the Lord hath commanded them. And after this manner of language did she speak.

9 And it came to pass that they did rejoice exceedingly, and did offer sacrifice and burnt offerings unto the Lord; and they gave thanks unto the God of Israel.

Their sons had returned. Lehi and Sariah were blessed with an increased testimony that God had not forgotten them. They became stronger together. What could have been a divorce or a marriage laden with heavy separatism was laced with greater strength and unity. By both looking to Heavenly Father, Lehi and Sariah further rendered themselves a new strength and yoked themselves together once more.

Their marriage was stronger. They were welded together with an even greater unity. Sometimes challenges in our marriages can be the very thing that makes us stronger—if we look to the Lord.

Answer: **Alma 41:10**

Commentary:

10 Do not suppose, because it has been spoken concerning restoration, that ye shall be restored from sin to happiness. Behold, I say unto you, wickedness never was happiness.

Simply stated, a marriage cannot be a happy one if there is anything in that marriage that has a wicked nature. The word "wicked" means "sinful, immoral, mean, foul, heinous, or dishonest." Its antonym is "virtuous, blameless, or principled." A happy marriage must be void of anything "wicked."

Answer: **1 Nephi 1:20**	Commentary:
. . . But behold, I, Nephi, will show unto you that the tender mercies of the Lord are over all those whom he hath chosen, because of their faith, to make them mighty even unto the power of deliverance.	*A happy marriage is one where each partner looks for, finds, and points out to the other the "tender mercies of the Lord" in their relationship, finances, friendships, leaders, profession, children, and so on. Looking for and always seeing the Lord's hand in our lives makes for a happy relationship. It is far too easy to find the problems, challenges, and rough spots. Finding a way to stay focused on blessings and tender mercies improves any marriage relationship and helps "deliver" us through the challenges.*

Answer: **2 Nephi 32: 2–5**	Commentary:
2 Do ye not remember that I said unto you that after ye had received the Holy Ghost ye could speak with the tongue of angels? And now, how could ye speak with the tongue of angels save it were by the Holy Ghost? 3 Angels speak by the power of the Holy Ghost; wherefore, they speak the words of Christ. Wherefore, I said unto you, feast upon the words of Christ; for behold, the words of Christ will tell you all things what ye should do.	*Improving a marriage is founded on whether or not the Lord and the Holy Ghost are in the relationship. If we want the Lord in the marriage relationship, it only stands to reason that "His Word" must be in it. Reading His word together, as well as in private, will do wonders. Nephi reminds us that as we "feast," or take-in the words of Christ, those words will tell us all the things we should do to improve the marriage.* *Nephi further reminds us that prayer— "asking Him"—is foundationally getting help and understanding. Praying together, as well as individually, is also a prerequisite for improving a marriage.*

4 Wherefore, now after I have spoken these words, if ye cannot understand them it will be because ye ask not, neither do ye knock; wherefore, ye are not brought into the light, but must perish in the dark.

5 For behold, again I say unto you that if ye will enter in by the way, and receive the Holy Ghost, it will show unto you all things what ye should do.

Finally, the Lord promises us that if we will pray to Heavenly Father in our marriage and read His word, He will tell us what to do to make the marriage stronger. The greatest part of the promise is that these things will qualify us for the Holy Ghost, who will show us all things we need to do to improve our marriage relationship.

Answer: **Moroni 7:44–48**

Commentary:

44 If so, his faith and hope is vain, for none is acceptable before God, save the meek and lowly in heart; and if a man be meek and lowly in heart, and confesses by the power of the Holy Ghost that Jesus is the Christ, he must needs have charity; for if he have not charity he is nothing; wherefore he must needs have charity.

45 And charity suffereth long, and is kind, and envieth not, and is not puffed up, seeketh not her own, is not easily provoked, thinketh no evil, and rejoiceth not in iniquity but rejoiceth in the truth, beareth all things, believeth all things, hopeth all things, endureth all things.

Sometimes when we think of charity, we equate it with visiting the sick, taking a casserole to some neighbor in need, or sharing our resources with the poor and the needy. However, charity is not something you give away; it is something you acquire or become. It is something that happens to the heart. Moroni admonishes us to pray for it with all our energy.

Charity is the foundation upon which every good marriage is built. "It suffereth long" (when things aren't going well, we suffer together). It is kind ("kindness" is defined as "gentle, helpful, considerate, selfless, concerned, warm, thoughtful, and understanding").

46 Wherefore, my beloved brethren, if ye have not charity, ye are nothing, for charity never faileth. Wherefore, cleave unto charity, which is the greatest of all, for all things must fail—

Charity doesn't "envy" (show bitterness or discontent). It doesn't "seek her own" (behave selfishly), and it "is not easily provoked' (doesn't generate or instigate contention). There is no "thinking evil." It bears tough times believing and hoping everything will work out in the end.

47 But charity is the pure love of Christ, and it endureth forever; and whoso is found possessed of it at the last day, it shall be well with him.

Marriages where each partner is striving to have the attribute of charity in their relationship will have sweet success. Charity is a purifying agent that will help change anything that is not good. It will support us when we have to bear or do hard things.

48 Wherefore, my beloved brethren, pray unto the Father with all the energy of heart, that ye may be filled with this love, which he hath bestowed upon all who are true followers of his Son, Jesus Christ; that ye may become the sons of God; that when he shall appear we shall be like him, for we shall see him as he is; that we may have this hope; that we may be purified even as he is pure. Amen.

Charity makes us become more like our Savior Jesus Christ.

QUESTION 7

How can I balance family, work, life, studies, church, responsibilities, and all the things I have to do?

Answer: **Mosiah 4:27**	Commentary:
27 And see that all these things are done in wisdom and order; for it is not requisite that a man should run faster than he has strength. And again, it is expedient that he should be diligent, that thereby he might win the prize; therefore, all things must be done in order.	*Most of us live in a world of calendars, appointments, and responsibilities. There is simply more to do than there is time to do it. Therefore, we must use wisdom to decide that which we leave undone in favor of that which must be done. Prioritizing is a process of using judgement and wisdom to put our lives into order. It is not thinking that we must do everything. Prioritizing gives us permission to leave some things undone. We have the responsibility to determine the essentials and to accomplish those.*

Answer: 3 Nephi 13:19–21, 33

19 Lay not up for yourselves treasures upon earth, where moth and rust doth corrupt, and thieves break through and steal;

20 But lay up for yourselves treasures in heaven, where neither moth nor rust doth corrupt, and where thieves do not break through nor steal.

21 For where your treasure is, there will your heart be also.

33 But seek ye first the kingdom of God and his righteousness, and all these things shall be added unto you.

Commentary:

Daily to-do lists and busy calendars are not easy to prioritize. Everything on our lists often seems important. Appointments might drive our lives.

When Jesus Christ visited the Americas, He taught that the most important thing we can do in this life is to seek the kingdom of God. If our activities and phantom priorities center around "earthly treasures"—seeking wealth and toys—at the expense of allowing our heart, interest, and time to be riveted to the matters of the Lord's kingdom, we should consider how we can make an adjustment. Heavenly Father has promised through his prophets that if we will put Him first, everything will fall into its proper place or drop out of our lives.

Answer: 2 Nephi 32:1, 3, 5

1 And now, behold, my beloved brethren, I suppose that ye ponder somewhat in your hearts concerning that which ye should do after ye have entered in by the way. But, behold, why do ye ponder these things in your hearts?

3 Angels speak by the power of the Holy Ghost; wherefore, they speak the words of Christ. Wherefore, I said unto you, feast upon the words of Christ; for behold, the words of

Commentary:

In the words of the Bible (Ecclesiastes 3:1–8) we are reminded that to everything there is a season—a time to be born, a time to die, a time to plant, a time to harvest, a time to kill and time to heal, a time to break down, and a time to build up. In this life there is a time to weep, a time to laugh, a time to mourn, and a time to dance. A time to cast away stones, a time to gather them, a time to embrace, and a time to avoid the embrace. A time to get, a time to lose, a time to keep, and a time

Christ will tell you all things what ye should do.

5 For behold, again I say unto you that if ye will enter in by the way, and receive the Holy Ghost, it will show unto you all things what ye should do.

to cast away. A time to rend, a time to sew, a time to be silent, and a time to speak. A time to love, a time to hate, a time of war, and a time of peace. In short, every stage of life is a "season," and we must do our best to do what needs to be done in each season.

Reading our scriptures, keeping the commandments, and being worthy of the Holy Ghost will help us know what needs to be done in each season. We should do our best and allow the impressions from the scriptures and the Holy Ghost to keep us in check.

QUESTION 8

Why is it that some people leave the Church because of being offended by another member or leader?

Answer: **Helaman 12:5**	Commentary:
5 Yea, how quick to be lifted up in pride; yea, how quick to boast, and do all manner of that which is iniquity; and how slow are they to remember the Lord their God, and to give ear unto his counsels, yea, how slow to walk in wisdom's paths!	*Being offended is a personal choice. People make the choice to be offended. The central issue in taking offense is pride. Perhaps people who take offense are looking at the imperfections of others instead of considering their own. Taking an offense to the actions or words of another could indicate that the offended isn't feeling very good about himself. To let go and forget the gospel and all of God's blessings and gifts is not a wise path.*

Answer: **2 Nephi 2:13–14**	Commentary:
13 And if ye shall say there is no law, ye shall also say there is no sin. If ye shall say there is no sin, ye shall also say there is no righteousness. And if there be no righteousness there be no happiness. And if there be no righteousness nor happiness there be no punishment nor misery. And if these things are not there is no God. And if there is no God we are not, neither the earth; for there could have been no creation of things, neither to act nor to be acted upon; wherefore, all things must have vanished away.	*We are children of a Heavenly Father who has blessed us with the gift of moral agency. We have the freedom to independently choose and act. The gift to all of His children allows us to act and not be acted upon. To believe or buy in to the idea that someone else can make us feel offended, hurt, bitter, or angry lessens our freedom to choose. It changes us into objects to be acted upon.*
	We have the power to choose how we will react to others in any given situation. If we allow the actions of others to impact how we act or react, then in reality we are more like puppets—and the other person is like a puppeteer who controls our every action.
14 And now, my sons, I speak unto you these things for your profit and learning; for there is a God, and he hath created all things, both the heavens and the earth, and all things that in them are, both things to act and things to be acted upon.	*It is important to act after the dictates of our beliefs and testimony, without being acted upon by the short-sighted comments or views of others.*

Answer: **1 Nephi 7:14**	Commentary:
14 For behold, the Spirit of the Lord ceaseth soon to strive with them; for behold, they have rejected the prophets, and Jeremiah have they cast into prison. And they have sought to take away the life of my father, insomuch that they have driven him out of the land.	*The price of taking offense and cutting ourselves off from the prophets or a bishop or other priesthood leader is great. We lose the Spirit by rejecting those whose calling it is to lead us.*
	Consider all the good that is lost through forsaking ordinances, temple blessings, being with a community of Saints, and other

great protections against Satan. That is what happens when we lose the Spirit of the Lord over an offense that is possibly not even intended.

Answer: **1 Nephi 2:11–12**	Commentary:
11 Now this he spake because of the stiffneckedness of Laman and Lemuel; for behold they did murmur in many things against their father, because he was a visionary man, and had led them out of the land of Jerusalem, to leave the land of their inheritance, and their gold, and their silver, and their precious things, to perish in the wilderness. And this they said he had done because of the foolish imaginations of his heart.	*Lehi moved his family from Jerusalem in order to save them from destruction. His two oldest sons murmured or "found fault" by being offended. Their murmurings would impact millions of their descendants. Many problems resulted from how Laman and Lemuel reacted to their father and from the bitterness they continued to teach to their children and grandchildren. Negative feelings and attitudes carried on for many centuries. We can easily see the result.*
12 And thus Laman and Lemuel, being the eldest, did murmur against their father. And they did murmur because they knew not the dealings of that God who had created them.	*Nephi noted an important cause of the offense in the first place. He observed, "they did murmur because they knew not the dealings of that God who had created them." Offense comes because we lose sight of the dealings of God and do not humbly seek to know them.*

QUESTION 9

How do I keep from becoming discouraged?

Answer: **Alma 37:35–37**	Commentary:
35 O, remember, my son, and learn wisdom in thy youth; yea, learn in thy youth to keep the commandments of God.	As Alma speaks to his son Helaman, he counsels him to remember the value of maintaining his connection to Heavenly Father through prayer.
36 Yea, and cry unto God for all thy support; yea, let all thy doings be unto the Lord, and whithersoever thou goest let it be in the Lord; yea, let all thy thoughts be directed unto the Lord; yea, let the affections of thy heart be placed upon the Lord forever.	Discouragement typically begins with worrying and wondering about how our external world (whatever it happens to be at the moment) impacts us individually. That viewpoint is selfish. It is "me" oriented.

| 37 Counsel with the Lord in all thy doings, and he will direct thee for good; yea, when thou liest down at night lie down unto the Lord, that he may watch over you in your sleep; and when thou risest in the morning let thy heart be full of thanks unto God; and if ye do these things, ye shall be lifted up at the last day. | *As we place our hearts and minds on the Lord and on the many blessings He has given us, we are more inclined to think less about ourselves. In turn, as we think less about ourselves, we are less discouraged.* |

Answer: **Mosiah 23:21–22**	Commentary:
21 Nevertheless the Lord seeth fit to chasten his people; yea, he trieth their patience and their faith.

22 Nevertheless—whosoever putteth his trust in him the same shall be lifted up at the last day. Yea, and thus it was with this people. | *When faced with discouragement, it is important to remember that "chastening" means "to purify and make clean." Therefore, our problems and challenges can be purifying and cleansing. The Lord tries or puts our patience to the test as a refining. This is the way of Heavenly Father.*

Ultimately the cleansing process requires that we put our trust in God. Trusting Heavenly Father who loves us becomes a great blessing.

Discouragement is an agent for learning to develop trust in God. |

Answer: **Ether 12:6**	Commentary:
6 And now, I, Moroni, would speak somewhat concerning these things; I would show unto the world that faith is things which are hoped for and not seen; wherefore, dispute not because ye see not, for ye	*Discouragement is often the by-product of loss of faith and hope. Moroni tells us that "understanding" or "a witness" will follow a trial of our faith and a challenge to our hope.*

| receive no witness until after the trial of your faith. | *Again the Lord seeks that we put our trust in Him. He knows all things.* |

Answer: **2 Nephi 9:20**

20 O how great the holiness of our God! For he knoweth all things, and there is not anything save he knows it.

Commentary:

Developing a trust in God must be very important. It is central to nearly every issue and concern. In discouraging moments, remember this great truth: Heavenly Father really does know all—and His primary purpose is to build us and help us to grow. That alone should be enough to move us to be more trusting in His judgment. All things in the economy of God will be consecrated for our good.

QUESTION 10

How do I deal with coworkers or friends who say negative things about or criticize the church?

Answer: **Alma 7:23**	Commentary:
23 And now I would that ye should be humble, and be submissive and gentle; easy to be entreated; full of patience and long-suffering; being temperate in all things; being diligent in keeping the commandments of God at all times; asking for whatsoever things ye stand in need, both spiritual and temporal; always returning thanks unto God for whatsoever things ye do receive.	*This question probably will come at some time into the heart of everyone who is a disciple of Christ. It is not easy to be ridiculed or mocked for what we believe. However, it is clear that we should exercise the attributes that Christ exhibited on His hard days of rejection and mocking—attributes of humility, submissiveness, patience, long suffering, temperance. Just "keep on keeping on" in keeping the commandments.*

Answer: **Mosiah 4:15**	Commentary:
15 But ye will teach them to walk in the ways of truth and soberness; ye will teach them to love one another, and to serve one another.	*King Benjamin, speaking to parents, taught that we should teach our children to keep the commandments by walking in the way of truth and soberness; we should teach them to love one another and "serve" one another. We can only teach what we ourselves are doing. Perhaps one of the best ways to deal with those who mock us is to serve them.*

Answer: **Alma 30:41**	Commentary:
41 But, behold, I have all things as a testimony that these things are true; and ye also have all things as a testimony unto you that they are true; and will ye deny them? Believest thou that these things are true?	*When we are criticized or made fun of, sometimes it all comes down to whether or not the things we believe in are true. In spite of all the hassle given by Korihor, Alma simply knew and had a testimony of the things he taught. In the end, that's all that mattered.*

Answers: **Mosiah 3:19**	Commentary:
19 For the natural man is an enemy to God, and has been from "the fall of Adam, and will be, forever and ever, unless he yields to the enticings of the Holy Spirit, and putteth off the natural man and becometh a saint through the atonement of Christ the Lord, and becometh as a child, submissive, meek, humble, patient, full of love, willing to submit to all things which the Lord seeth fit to inflict upon	*Dealing with difficult or negative people—people who scoff, scorn, and sneer at that which is true, good, and right—has been one of the challenges of every true disciple of Jesus Christ all through the annals of history. It's just a part of the turf! However, how we deal with negativity and agitation is important. We can't stoop to the ways of the "natural man," which is to retort or snap back. We must yield to the enticing*

him, even as a child doth submit to his father.	*of the Holy Spirit and put off the natural man. We must be submissive, meek, patient, full of love, and respond in a childlike (not childish) manner.*

Answer: **Alma 1:19–25**	Commentary:
19 But it came to pass that whosoever did not belong to the church of God began to persecute those that did belong to the church of God, and had taken upon them the name of Christ.	*This is a wonderful story for any true disciple of Christ who has a constant or a periodic challenge of dealing with people who jeer at sacred things—people who try to pull down those who are trying to live on a higher level.*
20 Yea, they did persecute them, and afflict them with all manner of words, and this because of their humility; because they were not proud in their own eyes, and because they did impart the word of God, one with another, without money and without price.	*The persecution became an intense war of words and a wrangling dispute.*
21 Now there was a strict law among the people of the church, that there should not any man, belonging to the church, arise and persecute those that did not belong to the church, and that there should be no persecution among themselves.	*Disputes arose even though there was a law that religion should not be a cause for any kind of persecution.*
22 Nevertheless, there were many among them who began to be proud, and began to contend warmly with their adversaries, even unto blows; yea, they would smite one another with their fists.	*The words turned to bare-knuckle fist fighting and physical assault.*

23 Now this was in the second year of the reign of Alma, and it was a cause of much affliction to the church; yea, it was the cause of much trial with the church.	*This became an issue or a challenge that was a burden and worry among the church members.*
24 For the hearts of many were hardened, and their names were blotted out, that they were remembered no more among the people of God. And also many withdrew themselves from among them.	*In this negative situation, church members who dissented and became a part of the problem were either excommunicated or simply withdrew themselves from the church and denied their faith.*
25 Now this was a great trial to those that did stand fast in the faith; nevertheless, they were steadfast and immovable in keeping the commandments of God, and they bore with patience the persecution which was heaped upon them.	*Now the reaction and response of the true disciples are recounted. Those true followers were committed, loyal, and secure in carrying on in their anchor of faith in Christ. They were patient and composed in their devotion to covenants made, in spite of tyranny and harassment. They would not be bullied away from the Savior but dealt with their plight calmly and unflappably.*

QUESTION 11

When I am faced with two options in the "road of life," how can I know which one to take?

Answer: **1 Nephi 15:7–11**	Commentary:
7 And they said: Behold, we cannot understand the words which our father hath spoken concerning the natural branches of the olive-tree, and also concerning the Gentiles. 8 And I said unto them: Have ye inquired of the Lord? 9 And they said unto me: We have not; for the Lord maketh no such thing known unto us.	*This question is one of the most universal questions of all. Every road, it seems, has a fork in it. It seems as though life is full of questions—roadblocks or opportunities, large and small, that demand we make choices regarding which road to take.* *Father Lehi and Nephi find their choices easier to make because they understand the doctrines—or "the whys"—associated with those choices. Laman and Lemuel constantly struggle because they don't understand. In a moment when the older brothers are struggling to understand with their heads or logic, Nephi poses a simple question in verse 8. He asks, "Have ye inquired of the Lord?"*

10 Behold, I said unto them: How is it that ye do not keep the commandments of the Lord? How is it that ye will perish, because of the hardness of your hearts?	*Laman and Lemuel respond, "No, because we don't get answers from the Lord." Our capacity to receive understanding about our forks in the road might come from having an attitude of doubt that we can, in fact, be given answers.*
11 Do ye not remember the things which the Lord hath said?—If ye will not harden your hearts, and ask me in faith, believing that ye shall receive, with diligence in keeping my commandments, surely these things shall be made known unto you.	*Then Nephi seeks to help his brothers understand that answers are predicated first upon keeping the commandments with diligence and being obedient to Heavenly Father's divine perspective.* *Understanding which road to take comes when we a) have faith and believe that we can receive answers b) keep the commandments and manifest our faith and belief with action, and c) ask Him!* *Father in Heaven desires to direct us in our choices but will never take away our agency to choose. Our part is in believing that we can get an answer, in acting, and in asking.*

Answer: **2 Nephi 31:17–21**	Commentary:
17 Wherefore, do the things which I have told you I have seen that your Lord and your Redeemer should do; for, for this cause have they been shown unto me, that ye might know the gate by which ye should enter. For the gate by which ye should enter is repentance and baptism by water; and then cometh a remission of your sins by fire and by the Holy Ghost.	*Making choices along the road or path of life is difficult much of the time. Nephi helps us understand that, in reality, there is only one path and one gate. When a fork in the road appears, Nephi explains that we follow the path to Christ! Repentance, baptism, and the receiving of the Holy Ghost.*

18 And then are ye in this strait and narrow path which leads to eternal life; yea, ye have entered in by the gate; ye have done according to the commandments of the Father and the Son; and ye have received the Holy Ghost, which witnesses of the Father and the Son, unto the fulfilling of the promise which he hath made, that if ye entered in by the way ye should receive.

19 And now, my beloved brethren, after ye have gotten into this strait and narrow path, I would ask if all is done? Behold, I say unto you, Nay; for ye have not come thus far save it were by the word of Christ with unshaken faith in him, relying wholly upon the merits of him who is mighty to save.

20 Wherefore, ye must press forward with a steadfastness in Christ, having a perfect brightness of hope, and a love of God and of all men. Wherefore, if ye shall press forward, feasting upon the word of Christ, and endure to the end, behold, thus saith the Father: Ye shall have eternal life.

21 And now, behold, my beloved brethren, this is the way; and there is none other way nor name given under heaven whereby man can be saved in the kingdom of God. And now, behold, this is the doctrine of Christ, and the only and true doctrine of the Father, and of the

Nephi explains that once we choose to repent daily, to keep our baptismal covenants, and to live in such a way as to allow the Holy Ghost to cleanse and burn out our sins, we set ourselves upon the correct path which is Christ the Lord. Then we move forward on that path. Our eyes are not focused on distracting options, but rather on the path of Christ.

As we keep our eyes on Christ, we find the journey well defined. Our trust in Him and His will are primary in our lives. We are more able to be directed by the Holy Ghost.

We must understand that intrusive and bothersome options will appear again and again as we go forth on the path.

The key is to understand that we must relentlessly keep moving our feet without compromise. Losing our focus will cost us! We maintain our trust in His way and commit to following Him on His timetable. Our love for Him prompts ever deepening confidence that He knows our dilemmas and concerns and will bless us through them.

He will coach us as we "feast upon the words of Christ" (the scriptures), stay attentive to counsel from the watchmen on the tower (His living prophets), and continue to move our feet forward.

Son, and of the Holy Ghost, which is one God, without end. Amen.	*Yes, there's just one road to follow. It is Christ!*
	Sound too simplistic? Following Him is based on action choices rooted in His plan for our happiness. Sometimes we might take a path that's not right. But with complete faith and trust in Him, He will help us to correct our course. When we take the correct road, He will verify and confirm our choice. There might be times when our choices between two paths are both good options; either path will keep us focused on Him. In His omniscience, He knows which path we will pursue. He will bless us for taking action and moving forward rather than being paralyzed by confusion and inaction.
	The choice (the road) is Christ! Because of our putting His will first, our exhibiting our pure trust in Him and His love for us, and our moving our faith to action, He will consecrate all things to our ultimate benefit.

Answer: **1 Nephi 18:1–5**	Commentary:
1 And it came to pass that they did worship the Lord, and did go forth with me; and we did work timbers of curious workmanship. And the Lord did show me from time to time after what manner I should work the timbers of the ship.	*Nephi and his family had traveled for eight hard years. Then they came to a land richly blessed with much fruit and wild honey. In their travels, the record states that "we had suffered many afflictions and much difficulty." Almost immediately after Nephi discovered this haven of rest with his family, the Lord asked him to go to the mountain where He commanded Nephi to build a ship.*

2 Now I, Nephi, did not work the timbers after the manner which was learned by men, neither did I build the ship after the manner of men; but I did build it after the manner which the Lord had shown unto me; wherefore, it was not after the manner of men.

3 And I, Nephi, did go into the mount oft, and I did pray oft unto the Lord; wherefore the Lord showed unto me great things.

4 And it came to pass that after I had finished the ship, according to the word of the Lord, my brethren beheld that it was good, and that the workmanship thereof was exceedingly fine; wherefore, they did humble themselves again before the Lord.

5 And it came to pass that the voice of the Lord came unto my father, that we should arise and go down into the ship.

Nephi used his agency to move forward, trusting in God. Though opposed by his brothers and their followers, he made tools and exhibited his faith with action.

Notice in verses 1–3 how Nephi's capacity to execute his choice came over time, and not all at once. In verse 1, "the Lord did show me from time to time." In verse 3, "I, Nephi, did go into the mount oft, and I did pray oft unto the Lord; wherefore the Lord showed unto me great things."

Sometimes when we come to the fork in the road, the answer regarding what we should do comes "from time to time," and only when the Lord is ready to show unto us great things.

In the end, Nephi's day-by-day diligence in taking instruction produced a ship—a good ship with "fine workmanship!" Letting the Lord dictate the answer in His own time and in His own way is a key to getting the right answer. As we move our feet forward, sometimes the answers come quickly and other times the answers come in carefully customized packets over time. Those day-by-day answers for Nephi produced a ship worthy of a voyage of significant distance and challenge.

Answer: **3 Nephi 13:31–34**	Commentary:
31 Therefore take no thought, saying, What shall we eat? or, What shall we drink? or, Wherewithal shall we be clothed? 32 For your heavenly Father knoweth that ye have need of all these things. 33 But seek ye first the kingdom of God and his righteousness, and all these things shall be added unto you. 34 Take therefore no thought for the morrow, for the morrow shall take thought for the things of itself. Sufficient is the day unto the evil thereof.	*The Savior states that many of our challenges with choice come as we try to make sense out of matters of the world. His ultimate counsel is that we realize that all decisions rest upon what we consider most important in life. Many of our earthly decisions have less importance than our motives toward our Father in Heaven.* *He promises that if we keep first things first, all else shall be added for our well being.* *Of course we must make necessary choices in the temporal affairs of our earthly lives. But putting God and His will appropriately before ours will always bless our choices in the other areas of our lives.*

Answer: **Moroni 7:16–17**	Commentary:
16 For behold, the Spirit of Christ is given to every man, that he may know good from evil; wherefore, I show unto you the way to judge; for every thing which inviteth to do good, and to persuade to believe in Christ, is sent forth by the power and gift of Christ; wherefore ye may know with a perfect knowledge it is of God.	*For all who are challenged with making appropriate decisions between multiple paths, Moroni gives a key—a way to judge.* *As we carefully consider our options, we ask of each road, "Does the road in front of me invite goodness and the belief in Christ and His will?" Further, "Does this road persuade me to do good, or are there hazards that will invite me to compromise the commandments in anyway?"*

17 But whatsoever thing persuadeth men to do evil, and believe not in Christ, and deny him, and serve not God, then ye may know with a perfect knowledge it is of the devil; for after this manner doth the devil work, for he persuadeth no man to do good, no, not one; neither do his angels; neither do they who subject themselves unto him.

Sometimes the examination of both roads suggests the same answer. If it leads us away from Christ, it should be hastily dismissed. If one or the other invites us to do good, then it can be embraced.

QUESTION 12

How can I maintain the capacity and ability to accomplish all that is expected of me?

Answer: **Alma 43**
(The whole chapter, with highlighted verses as indicated below)

4 For behold, it came to pass that the Zoramites became Lamanites; therefore, in the commencement of the eighteenth year the people of the Nephites saw that the Lamanites were coming upon them; therefore they made preparations for war; yea, they gathered together their armies in the land of Jershon.

16 Now, the leader of the Nephites, or the man who had been appointed took the command of all the armies of the Nephites—and his name was Moroni;

Commentary:

Chapter 43 is a wonderful trilogy to answer this "question of the soul" through the example of Captain Moroni.

This great military leader understood what it takes to have and maintain the power to accomplish. He must have understood that mankind is spurred to action by human motivations. Nearly everyone can trace their actions to these three: fear, duty, and love. Sometimes we act because we fear that if we don't, we will reap a negative consequence. If we are employed and don't show up for work, we get fired; if we expose ourselves to tobacco smoke, we might get cancer; if we are not nice to other people, we might lose favor with all of them; and so forth.

17 And Moroni took all the command, and the government of their wars. And he was only twenty and five years old when he was appointed chief captain over the armies of the Nephites.

18 And it came to pass that he met the Lamanites in the borders of Jershon, and his people were armed with swords, and with cimeters, and all manner of weapons of war.

19 And when the armies of the Lamanites saw that the people of Nephi, or that Moroni, had prepared his people with breastplates and with arm-shields, yea, and also shields to defend their heads, and also they were dressed with thick clothing—

20 Now the army of Zerahemnah was not prepared with any such thing; they had only their swords and their cimeters, their bows and their arrows, their stones and their slings; and they were naked, save it were a skin which was girded about their loins; yea, all were naked, save it were the Zoramites and the Amalekites;

21 But they were not armed with breastplates, nor shields—therefore, they were exceedingly afraid of the armies of the Nephites because of their armor, notwithstanding their

Another motivation is "duty." We are motivated to action because it is our responsibility or duty to do something. We go to church because we feel it is our obligation to as Latter-day Saints. We help with school programs to show our allegiance, or we attend training meetings for cub or boy scouts because we committed to serve others.

The third and highest form of human motivation is "love." We serve our family because we love them. We go on missions because we love the Savior and the people that we teach.

A quick read of the whole chapter will help in understanding the background of this wonderful story. Suffice it to say that Nephite defectors joined forces with the enemy, the Lamanites. Moroni prepared his armies with body shields, weapons, and military strategy. The enemy, despite being more numerous, were not as well prepared.

number being so much greater than the Nephites.

22 Behold, now it came to pass that they durst not come against the Nephites in the borders of Jershon; therefore they departed out of the land of Antionum into the wilderness, and took their journey round about in the wilderness, away by the head of the river Sidon, that they might come into the land of Manti and take possession of the land; for they did not suppose that the armies of Moroni would know whither they had gone.

23 But it came to pass, as soon as they had departed into the wilderness Moroni sent spies into the wilderness to watch their camp; and Moroni, also, knowing of the prophecies of Alma, sent certain men unto him, desiring him that he should inquire of the Lord whither the armies of the Nephites should go to defend themselves against the Lamanites.

24 And it came to pass that the word of the Lord came unto Alma, and Alma informed the messengers of Moroni, that the armies of the Lamanites were marching round about in the wilderness, that they might come over into the land of Manti, that they might commence an attack upon the weaker part of the people. And those messengers

Moroni had obtained information from spies and from the Prophet Alma regarding the plan of attack of the Lamanites and Nephite dissenters (called Zoramites).

went and delivered the message unto Moroni.

25 Now Moroni, leaving a part of his army in the land of Jershon, lest by any means a part of the Lamanites should come into that land and take possession of the city, took the remaining part of his army and marched over into the land of Manti.

Moroni developed a counter plan—utilizing the Hill Riplah, the River Sidon, and a Valley—to preserve his people and, at the same time, defeat or repel the enemy. The plan was executed with precision, and the enemies found themselves close to a grand defeat. It looked as though the Nephites were going to be victorious on every count.

26 And he caused that all the people in that quarter of the land should gather themselves together to battle against the Lamanites, to defend their lands and their country, their rights and their liberties; therefore they were prepared against the time of the coming of the Lamanites.

27 And it came to pass that Moroni caused that his army should be secreted in the valley which was near the bank of the river Sidon, which was on the west of the river Sidon in the wilderness.

28 And Moroni placed spies round about, that he might know when the camp of the Lamanites should come.

37 And the work of death commenced on both sides, but it was more dreadful on the part of the Lamanites, for their nakedness

was exposed to the heavy blows of the Nephites with their swords and their cimeters, which brought death almost at every stroke.

44 And they were inspired by the Zoramites and the Amalekites, who were their chief captains and leaders, and by Zerahemnah, who was their chief captain, or their chief leader and commander; yea, they did fight like dragons, and many of the Nephites were slain by their hands, yea, for they did smite in two many of their head-plates, and they did pierce many of their breast-plates, and they did smite off many of their arms; and thus the Lamanites did smite in their fierce anger.

48 And it came to pass that when the men of Moroni saw the fierceness and the anger of the Lamanites, they were about to shrink and flee from them. And Moroni, perceiving their intent, sent forth and inspired their hearts with these thoughts— yea, the thoughts of their lands, their liberty, yea, their freedom from bondage.

49 And it came to pass that they turned upon the Lamanites, and they cried with one voice unto the Lord their God, for their liberty and their freedom from bondage.

Then the Lamanites "fear motivation" kicked in! They fought like dragons, and very quickly the battle turned on the Nephites. Instead of holding the upper hand, the Nephites were on the verge of losing this key battle.

The Nephites were about to retreat and give up.

However, Moroni knew the answer to the question, "How can I maintain the capacity and ability to accomplish all that is expected of me?"

He knew that capacity and the real under-pinnings of victory lay not in how the battle was fought or what the strategy was. Power and sustainability comes from "the why." Moroni reminded his men that the battle was not about blood, headplates, or breastplates. The battle was about their homes, their children, and their liberty. That is why they were fighting.

Notice what happened! The Nephites rallied and won, even though they were out-numbered two to one.

The answer to the question, "How can I maintain the capacity and ability to ac-complish all that is expected of me?" is found in "the why." It is not found in fear or in duty. It is found in love.

50 And they began to stand against the Lamanites with power; and in that selfsame hour that they cried unto the Lord for their freedom, the Lamanites began to flee before them; and they fled even to the waters of Sidon.

Finding and staying focused on our "why" and being motivated by love yields capacity and ability. Focusing solely on "what" and "how" or finding our motivation in "duty" and "fear" creates a loss of power.

Answer: **Alma 46**
(all of the chapter with highlights from the following verses)

4 And Amalickiah was desirous to be a king; and those people who were wroth were also desirous that he should be their king; and they were the greater part of them the lower judges of the land, and they were seeking for power.

7 And there were many in the church who believed in the flattering words of Amalickiah, therefore they dissented even from the church; and thus were the affairs of the people of Nephi exceedingly precarious and dangerous, notwithstanding their great victory which they had had over the Lamanites, and their great rejoicings which they had had because of their deliverance by the hand of the Lord.

8 Thus we see how quick the children of men do forget the Lord their God, yea, how quick to do

Commentary:

Fast forward one year from the story above. Captain Moroni was enjoying relative peace with the Lamanites in a military sense. However, there was a different kind of battle going on: a battle of governmental philosophy. A man by the name of Amalickiah desired to be king in a land where democracy and the voice of the people had prevailed for a number of years.

Amalickiah was leading many away, and was exercising much influence over the masses.

iniquity, and to be led away by the evil one.

9 Yea, and we also see the great wickedness one very wicked man can cause to take place among the children of men.

10 Yea, we see that Amalickiah, because he was a man of cunning device and a man of many flattering words, that he led away the hearts of many people to do wickedly; yea, and to seek to destroy the church of God, and to destroy the foundation of liberty which God had granted unto them, or which blessing God had sent upon the face of the land for the righteous' sake.

11 And now it came to pass that when Moroni, who was the chief commander of the armies of the Nephites, had heard of these dissensions, he was angry with Amalickiah.

Moroni turned again to his understanding of the power of purpose, the "why," and of the powerful motivator of love.

12 And it came to pass that he rent his coat; and he took a piece thereof, and wrote upon it—In memory of our God, our religion, and freedom, and our peace, our wives, and our children—and he fastened it upon the end of a pole.

Moroni wrote down the "whys" for the Nephites and the reasons that caused them to love God, religion, freedom, their wives, and their children.

13 And he fastened on his head-plate, and his breastplate, and his shields, and girded on his armor about his loins; and he took the pole, which had on the end thereof his rent coat, (and he called it the title of liberty) and he bowed himself to the earth, and he prayed mightily unto his God for the blessings of liberty to rest upon his brethren, so long as there should a band of Christians remain to possess the land—

There was no military war being waged; this was peacetime. In a symbolic act, Moroni put on his headgear and breastplate and took his shield, armour, and the title of liberty, which bore the "whys" and reasons in writing. He went among the people to remind them of what they had at stake.

19 And when Moroni had said these words, he went forth among the people, waving the rent part of his garment in the air, that all might see the writing which he had written upon the rent part, and crying with a loud voice, saying:

Can you imagine this?

20 Behold, whosoever will maintain this title upon the land, let them come forth in the strength of the Lord, and enter into a covenant that they will maintain their rights, and their religion, that the Lord God may bless them.

The people were duly reminded and invited to recommit to the higher principles associated with their system of government.

The dramatic impact of reminding people of their reasons changed their focus quickly and sustainably.

21 And it came to pass that when Moroni had proclaimed these words, behold, the people came running together with their armor girded about their loins, rending their garments in token, or as a covenant, that they would not forsake the Lord their God; or, in other words, if they should transgress the commandments of God, or fall into

The question, "How can I maintain the capacity and ability to accomplish all that is expected of me?" is a universally important question of the soul. How can we have the capacity and ability to be leaders, missionaries, parents, and students while playing multiple roles with various sets of expectations? When we focus

transgression, and be ashamed to take upon them the name of Christ, the Lord should rend them even as they had rent their garments.

22 Now this was the covenant which they made, and they cast their garments at the feet of Moroni, saying: We covenant with our God, that we shall be destroyed, even as our brethren in the land northward, if we shall fall into transgression; yea, he may cast us at the feet of our enemies, even as we have cast our garments at thy feet to be trodden under foot, if we shall fall into transgression.

23 Moroni said unto them: Behold, we are a remnant of the seed of Jacob; yea, we are a remnant of the seed of Joseph, whose coat was rent by his brethren into many pieces; yea, and now behold, let us remember to keep the commandments of God, or our garments shall be rent by our brethren, and we be cast into prison, or be sold, or be slain.

on "whats" and "hows," our "whys" might become significantly diminished, and our power to perform is reduced.

When we forget why we are leaders, missionaries, parents, students, and all the other roles we play, we are more susceptible to failure and disappointment.

Answer: **Alma 62:4–5**

4 And he did raise the standard of liberty in whatsoever place he did enter, and gained whatsoever force he could in all his march towards the land of Gideon.

Commentary:

Even a dozen years later, Captain Moroni used the standard of liberty (the statement of "whys") to help.

This engaging series of stories featuring Captain Moroni demonstrate why Mormon wrote of him:

l it came to pass that thousands did flock unto his standard, and did take up their swords in the defence of their freedom, that they might not come into bondage.

"Yea, and he was a man who was firm in the faith of Christ, and he had sworn with an oath to defend his people, his rights, and his country, and his religion, even to the loss of his blood" (Alma 48:13).

"Yea, verily, verily I say unto you, if all men had been, and were, and ever would be, like unto Moroni, behold, the very powers of hell would have been shaken forever; yea, the devil would never have power over the hearts of the children of men" (Alma 48:17).

Christ is power. In Christ, we can have the capacity and ability to do all that is expedient. Finding Him and remembering to make Him our great "why" will give us the "love" (even charity, or His pure love) to be sufficient in whatever roles we are asked to perform.

QUESTION 13

Is there a God?

Answer: **Alma 22**
(all of the chapter with highlights from the following verses)

5 Now the king said unto them: What is this that ye have said concerning the Spirit of the Lord? Behold, this is the thing which doth trouble me.

6 And also, what is this that Ammon said—If ye will repent ye shall be saved, and if ye will not repent, ye shall be cast off at the last day?

7 And Aaron answered him and said unto him: Believest thou that there is a God? And the king said: I know that the Amalekites say that there is a God, and I have

Commentary:

Through all the ages of time, people have asked a fundamental question relative to the existence of God. Is there a God or not? The atheist denounces God altogether, saying there is no God. Period! Others are agnostics—skeptics and doubters who become very cynical about the possibility of anything greater than mankind. They rely on logic and intellect. It is not clear in this story what "the king" believes, but it seems obvious that he is searching for an answer about the existence of God. There is a difference between wanting to know there is a God in Heaven and fighting against the possibility or searching for evidence to prove there is no supreme being.

granted unto them that they should build sanctuaries, that they may assemble themselves together to worship him. And if now thou sayest there is a God, behold I will believe.

In the early part of the story, the king states that the Amalekites believe there is a God and that he has allowed them to worship, even though he shares no conviction or personal investment in such. However, his confidence in Aaron has grown to a point where he is ready to believe.

8 And now when Aaron heard this, his heart began to rejoice, and he said: Behold, assuredly as thou livest, O king, there is a God.

Elder Robert D. Hales gave helpful commentary on this subject when he stated, "As prophesied, we live in a time when the darkness of secularism is deepening around us. Belief in God is widely questioned and even attacked in the name of political, social, and even religious causes. Atheism, or the doctrine that there is no God, is fast spreading across the world.

"Even so, as members of the restored Church of Jesus Christ, we declare that 'we believe in God, the Eternal Father, and in His Son, Jesus Christ, and in the Holy Ghost.'

"Some wonder, 'Why is belief in God so important?' Why did the Savior say, 'And this is life eternal, that they might know thee the only true God, and Jesus Christ, whom thou hast sent'?

"Without God, life would end at the grave, and our mortal experiences would have no purpose. Growth and progress would be temporary, accomplishment without value, challenges without meaning. There would be no ultimate right or wrong and no moral responsibility to care for one another as fellow children of God. Indeed, without God, there would be no mortal or eternal life.

9 And the king said: Is God that Great Spirit that brought our fathers out of the land of Jerusalem?

10 And Aaron said unto him: Yea, he is that Great Spirit, and he created all things both in heaven and in earth. Believest thou this?

11 And he said: Yea, I believe that the Great Spirit created all things, and I desire that ye should tell me concerning all these things, and I will believe thy words.

17 And it came to pass that when Aaron had said these words, the king did bow down before the Lord, upon his knees; yea, even he did prostrate himself upon the earth, and cried mightily, saying:

18 O God, Aaron hath told me that there is a God; and if there is a God, and if thou art God, wilt thou make thyself known unto me, and I will give away all my sins to know thee, and that I may be raised from the dead, and be saved at the last day. And now when the king had said these words, he was struck as if he were dead.

"If you or someone you love is seeking purpose in life or a deeper conviction of God's presence in our lives, I offer, as a friend and as an Apostle, my witness. He lives!

"Some may ask, 'How can I know this for myself?' We know He lives because we believe the testimonies of His ancient and living prophets, and we have felt God's Spirit confirm that the testimonies of these prophets are true.

"From their testimonies, recorded in holy scripture, we know that '[God] created man, male and female, after his own image and in his own likeness.' Some people may be surprised to learn that we look like God. One prominent religious scholar has even taught that imagining God in the form of man is creating a graven image and is idolatrous and blasphemous. But God Himself said, 'Let us make man in our image, after our likeness.'

"Gaining this knowledge is ultimately the quest of all God's children on the earth. If you cannot remember believing in God or if you have ceased to believe or if you believe but without real conviction, I invite you to seek a testimony of God now. Do not be afraid of ridicule. The strength and peace that come from knowing God and having the comforting companionship of His Spirit will make your efforts eternally worthwhile." (Robert D. Hales, "Seeking to know God, Our Heavenly Father, and His Son, Jesus Christ," *CR*, Oct. 2009.)

Answer: **Alma 30**
(all of the chapter, with highlights from the following verses)

37 And then Alma said unto him:
Believest thou that there is a God?

38 And he answered, Nay.

39 Now Alma said unto him: Will
ye deny again that there is a God,
and also deny the Christ? For behold, I say unto you, I know there
is a God, and also that Christ shall
come.

40 And now what evidence have ye
that there is no God, or that Christ
cometh not? I say unto you that ye
have none, save it be your word only.

41 But, behold, I have all things as
a testimony that these things are
true; and ye also have all things as a
testimony unto you that they are
true; and will ye deny them?
Believest thou that these things are
true?

42 Behold, I know that thou
believest, but thou art possessed
with a lying spirit, and ye have put
off the Spirit of God that it may
have no place in you; but the devil
has power over you, and he doth
carry you about, working devices
that he may destroy the children of
God.

Commentary:

*This is the story of Korihor. Not only did
he deny belief in God, but he ridiculed the
Savior, the Atonement, and the spirit of
prophecy—falsely teaching that there is
no God and no Christ.*

*Korihor was not satisfied to merely reject
God and quietly make his own conclusion.
Instead, he mocked the believers and demanded that the prophet Alma convince
him of God's existence and power with a
sign.*

*In a significant verbal interchange, Ko-
rihor scoffingly demanded proof of God's
existence. Alma responded with a recipro-
cal, "And now what evidence have ye that
there is no God?"*

*Alma stated with boldness that close ob-
servation shows a plethora of indications
and testaments of the existence of God.*

43 And now Korihor said unto Alma: If thou wilt show me a sign, that I may be convinced that there is a God, yea, show unto me that he hath power, and then will I be convinced of the truth of thy words.

Korihor demanded more obvious and personal evidence to convince him to become a believer.

44 But Alma said unto him: Thou hast had signs enough; will ye tempt your God? Will ye say, Show unto me a sign, when ye have the testimony of all these thy brethren, and also all the holy prophets? The scriptures are laid before thee, yea, and all things denote there is a God; yea, even the earth, and all things that are upon the face of it, yea, and its motion, yea, and also all the planets which move in their regular form do witness that there is a Supreme Creator.

Alma gave Korihor another opportunity to consider the many testaments of the existence of God. He invited this man of godless intent to simply open his eyes and consider what he sees: trees, grass, insects, ecosystems of perfect order, the moon, and the stars. Consider the impact each has on the beauty and order of things on earth. Consider oxygen to breath in the perfect combination of gasses and food to eat in the perfect blend to sustain mankind. Alma invited Korihor to consider the witnesses of all things.

45 And yet do ye go about, leading away the hearts of this people, testifying unto them there is no God? And yet will ye deny against all these witnesses? And he said: Yea, I will deny, except ye shall show me a sign.

Still Korihor wanted more evidence!

46 And now it came to pass that Alma said unto him: Behold, I am grieved because of the hardness of your heart, yea, that ye will still resist the spirit of the truth, that thy soul may be destroyed.

47 But behold, it is better that thy soul should be lost than that thou

shouldst be the means of bringing many souls down to destruction, by thy lying and by thy flattering words; therefore if thou shalt deny again, behold God shall smite thee, that thou shalt become dumb, that thou shalt never open thy mouth any more, that thou shalt not deceive this people any more.

48 Now Korihor said unto him: I do not deny the existence of a God, but I do not believe that there is a God; and I say also, that ye do not know that there is a God; and except ye show me a sign, I will not believe.

49 Now Alma said unto him: This will I give unto thee for a sign, that thou shalt be struck dumb, according to my words; and I say, that in the name of God, ye shall be struck dumb, that ye shall no more have utterance.

Korihor got his evidence.

50 Now when Alma had said these words, Korihor was struck dumb, that he could not have utterance, according to the words of Alma.

59 And it came to pass that as he went forth among the people, yea, among a people who had separated themselves from the Nephites and called themselves Zoramites, being led by a man whose name was Zoram—and as he went forth amongst them, behold, he was run

Korihor lived a rather pathetic life with a curse that was never taken from him. He was ultimately trampled to death by a group of people who claimed superiority in their own relationship to God.

upon and trodden down, even until he was dead.

60 And thus we see the end of him who perverteth the ways of the Lord; and thus we see that the devil will not support his children at the last day, but doth speedily drag them down to hell.

Coming to know that there is a God, that He is our Father, and that He loves us is an individual endeavor. It generally is not proved with signs or dramatic experiences. It is most often achieved by considering those evidences around us that denote supreme intelligence and absolute understanding of all things.

QUESTION 14
Why must I make hard decisions?

Answer: **2 Nephi 2:11, 15–16, 27**	Commentary:
11 For it must needs be, that there is an opposition in all things. If not so, my first-born in the wilderness, righteousness could not be brought to pass, neither wickedness, neither holiness nor misery, neither good nor bad. Wherefore, all things must needs be a compound in one; wherefore, if it should be one body it must needs remain as dead, having no life neither death, nor corruption nor incorruption, happiness nor misery, neither sense nor insensibility.	*Part of earthly life is opposition. In our premortal and mortal existences, we have been given the power to make choices between opposing options.*
	Because there is choice, we are given agency, or the right to select between good and evil. Sometimes our options even between good and good or good and better. But still we choose.
15 And to bring about his eternal purposes in the end of man, after he had created our first parents, and the beasts of the field and the fowls of the air, and in fine, all things which	

are created, it must needs be that there was an opposition; even the forbidden fruit in opposition to the tree of life; the one being sweet and the other bitter.

16 Wherefore, the Lord God gave unto man that he should act for himself. Wherefore, man could not act for himself save it should be that he was enticed by the one or the other.

While the rest of Heavenly Father's creations operate on genetic coding or hormonal indicators, as offspring of God we are given to act for ourselves. To choose.

27 Wherefore, men are free according to the flesh; and all things are given them which are expedient unto man. And they are free to choose liberty and eternal life, through the great Mediator of all men, or to choose captivity and death, according to the captivity and power of the devil; for he seeketh that all men might be miserable like unto himself.

We are free to choose the right and receive the blessings, or choose captivity and receive the consequences. When our choices lead us to captivity, our power to choose is diminished. But even then we can choose how we react in that captivity.

Answer: **Mosiah 2:21**

21 I say unto you that if ye should serve him who has created you from the beginning, and is preserving you from day to day, by lending you breath, that ye may live and move and do according to your own will, and even supporting you from one moment to another—I say, if ye should serve him with all your whole souls yet ye would be unprofitable servants.

Commentary:

King Benjamin addressed his people, counseling them to choose to serve God of their own will. To compel or force us to do good was the alternative that Lucifer proposed, contrary to God's plan.

Fundamental to life is the gift to choose "according to [our] own will."

Answer: **Alma 12:31**	Commentary:
31 Wherefore, he gave commandments unto men, they having first transgressed the first commandments as to things which were temporal, and becoming as Gods, knowing good from evil, placing themselves in a state to act, or being placed in a state to act according to their wills and pleasures, whether to do evil or to do good—	*We are given the power to act and not to be acted upon. It is a fundamental gift from Heavenly Father to choose good over evil according to our own will and pleasure. To choose between good and evil was, is, and will be a gift never to be taken from us.*

Answer: **Helaman 14:30**	Commentary:
30 And now remember, remember, my brethren, that whosoever perisheth, perisheth unto himself; and whosoever doeth iniquity, doeth it unto himself; for behold, ye are free; ye are permitted to act for yourselves; for behold, God hath given unto you a knowledge and he hath made you free.	*The old adage, "What goes around comes around," is true of agency. With our freedom to choose, we "doeth it" to ourselves. We make choices and act upon them. However, we are not free to choose the consequences. Our agency gives us choice, and our choices bring us consequences according to the choices we make.*

QUESTION 15
Why am I here on earth?

Answer: **Alma 42:4**

4 And thus we see, that there was a time granted unto man to repent, yea, a probationary time, a time to repent and serve God.

Commentary:

Heavenly Father gives us a span of time to change from our natural state and to demonstrate our capacity to choose good over evil. "Probation" means "the process or period of testing or observing the character or abilities of a person." "Repent" means "to change or turn around." Earthly life is exactly that; it's a time to change from our natural, physical nature and turn around to become who we really are as spiritual sons and daughters of God. It's a time to be tested and observed. It's a time to change from our self-serving ways and develop a desire to be grateful servants of Him who gave us life!

Answer: **Mosiah 3:19**	Commentary:
19 For the natural man is an enemy to God, and has been from the fall of Adam, and will be, forever and ever, unless he yields to the enticings of the Holy Spirit, and putteth off the natural man and becometh a saint through the atonement of Christ the Lord, and becometh as a child, submissive, meek, humble, patient, full of love, willing to submit to all things which the Lord seeth fit to inflict upon him, even as a child doth submit to his father.	*We are given earthly life to "put off the natural man and become a saint through the atonement of Christ the Lord." This life is intended to be a time for us to learn to take on the qualities of our Lord and Savior and cease to be an enemy to God our Creator.* *Becoming childlike is a lifelong task. Learning to be submissive, gentle, tamed, and self disciplined—to do what Heavenly Father wants for us over what we want for ourselves—is a challenge that takes time. Our mortal life is that time.*

Answer: **Alma 12:31–33**	Commentary:
31 Wherefore, he gave commandments unto men, they having first transgressed the first commandments as to things which were temporal, and becoming as Gods, knowing good from evil, placing themselves in a state to act, or being placed in a state to act according to their wills and pleasures, whether to do evil or to do good—	*We are on earth to learn of the commandments our God and Creator gave to us and then to keep or live according to them.* *God gave us the power to choose, knowing good from evil.*
32 Therefore God gave unto them commandments, after having made known unto them the plan of redemption, that they should not do evil, the penalty thereof being a second death, which was an everlasting death as to things pertaining	*He has given us His plan to overcome the consequences of the fall of Adam.*

unto righteousness; for on such the plan of redemption could have no power, for the works of justice could not be destroyed, according to the supreme goodness of God.

33 But God did call on men, in the name of his Son, (this being the plan of redemption which was laid) saying: If ye will repent, and harden not your hearts, then will I have mercy upon you, through mine Only Begotten Son;

Answer: **Alma 34:32**

32 For behold, this life is the time for men to prepare to meet God; yea, behold the day of this life is the day for men to perform their labors.

Commentary:

We are on earth to prepare to meet God. It is the entire purpose of our existence—to live life so that we can return to and become like Him. It is a time to perform and learn to act as He has prescribed. His way is the only way to eternal joy, and His greatest goal is our happiness.

QUESTION 16
What is the purpose of my life?

Answer: **Alma 34:32**	Commentary:
32 For behold, this life is the time for men to prepare to meet God; yea, behold the day of this life is the day for men to perform their labors.	*Heavenly Father has a plan for us. He wants us to qualify to return to Him and be as He is. This life is a time to do all that it takes to prepare ourselves to accomplish that. Earth is a place where we can receive a body, exercise our agency to make choices, make eternal covenants, and receive critical ordinances.*

Answer: **2 Nephi 2:25, 27–28**	Commentary:
25 Adam fell that men might be; and men are, that they might have joy.	*Lehi explains that, because of the Fall of Adam, the channel was opened for God's children to come to earth. We exist to have joy, which comes through living according to Heavenly Father's Plan.*
27 Wherefore, men are free according to the flesh; and call things are given them which are expedient unto man. And they are free to choose liberty and eternal life, through the great Mediator of all men, or to choose captivity and death, according to the captivity and power of the devil; for he seeketh that all men might be miserable like unto himself.	*The road to joy and happiness versus sorrow and pain pivots upon the way each of us uses his agency. God's children are free to choose with their own will God's Plan and happiness or Satan's plan and captivity. Lucifer is miserable; his objective is to spoil man's quest for joy and happiness and to make them feel the same misery he endlessly experiences.*
28 And now, my sons, I would that ye should look to the great Mediator, and hearken unto his great commandments; and be faithful unto his words, and choose eternal life, according to the will of his Holy Spirit;	*The only way we can experience the joy and happiness available to us now and through the eternities is through coming unto Jesus Christ and remaining true and faithful to Him and the Father.*

Answer: **2 Nephi 2:21–24**	Commentary:
21 And the days of the children of men were prolonged, according to the will of God, that they might repent while in the flesh; wherefore, their state became a state of probation, and their time was lengthened, according to the commandments which the Lord God gave unto the children of men. For he gave commandment that all men	*One of the fundamental purposes of life is to change or repent while we are living here on earth. Because of the effects of the Fall, we sin and make many mistakes. The Atonement of Jesus Christ makes it possible for us to repent and execute the change necessary for us to return to our Father in Heaven by living according to His commandments.*

must repent; for he showed unto all men that they were lost, because of the transgression of their parents.

22 And now, behold, if Adam had not transgressed he would not have fallen, but he would have remained in the garden of Eden. And all things which were created must have remained in the same state in which they were after they were created; and they must have remained forever, and had no end.

The Fall of Adam and Eve was a critically important step in Heavenly Father's Plan of Happiness. It was essential to our progress.

23 And they would have had no children; wherefore they would have remained in a state of innocence, having no joy, for they knew no misery; doing no good, for they knew no sin.

Joy is possible only because of the misery introduced by the Fall of Adam. Joy and happiness are possible by being true and faithful to the commandments given by Heavenly Father to help us overcome sin and the effects of the Fall.

24 But behold, all things have been done in the wisdom of him who knoweth all things.

Answer: **Mosiah 2:17**

Commentary:

17 And behold, I tell you these things that ye may learn wisdom; that ye may learn that when ye are in the service of your fellow beings ye are only in the service of your God.

Service is an essential part of our purpose on earth. The Savior led the way by example. We are invited to look outside ourselves and understand that loving and serving our fellow man is one of things we came to earth to learn. There is a tendency for God's children to be self absorbed in a world that asks, "What's in it for me?" We are invited to turn that around and become anxiously engaged in serving those around us.

Answer: **Mosiah 5:15**

15 Therefore, I would that ye should be steadfast and immovable, always abounding in good works, that Christ, the Lord God Omnipotent, may seal you his, that you may be brought to heaven, that ye may have everlasting salvation and eternal life, through the wisdom, and power, and justice, and mercy of him who created all things, in heaven and in earth, who is God above all. Amen.

Commentary:

The purpose of life includes "abounding in good works," and one of those works is to show our faith in Jesus Christ. It is necessary to develop a constant focus on the Father and the Son, rather than an episodic, irregular, or occasional focus.

"Steadfast" means "to be loyal, faithful, committed, devoted, dedicated, dependable, reliable, steady, true, constant, staunch, solid, and trusting."

"Immovable" means "to be fixed, secure, stable, moored, anchored, rooted, braced, set firm, or set fast."

Our purpose is to become steadfast and immovable.

QUESTION 17
What is the purpose of death?

Answer: **2 Nephi 9:6**	Commentary:
6 For as death hath passed upon all men, to fulfil the merciful plan of the great Creator, there must needs be a power of resurrection, and the resurrection must needs come unto man by reason of the fall; and the fall came by reason of transgression; and because man became fallen they were cut off from the presence of the Lord.	*Just as we were born into mortality, we will leave mortality through death. It is a crucial part of Heavenly Father's Plan. Christ could not be resurrected until He died. We too cannot be resurrected and receive the full measure of the joy that will come to us in the eternal perspective until we die.* *Death is a passage from this life into the next, just as birth is a passage or transition from our premortal life to life on earth. There is a perfect design in this progressive process.*

Answer: **Mosiah 16:7–8**	Commentary:
7 And if Christ had not risen from the dead, or have broken the bands of death that the grave should have no victory, and that death should have no sting, there could have been no resurrection.	*When someone we love dies, it is difficult for us. We love them and will miss them. Abinadi calls this a "sting" of death. The word "sting" means "heartache, heartbreak, agony, torture, torment, hurt, pain, or anguish."*
8 But there is a resurrection, therefore the grave hath no victory, and the sting of death is swallowed up in Christ.	*Because of Jesus Christ and His resurrection, death loses its sting. Agony, torture, and pain can be decreased knowing that the grave is not the end, but rather a new beginning. Heartache, torment, hurt, and anguish are lessened in knowing that Christ's resurrection consumed and put away the sting because all will live again. In fact, those departed loved ones continue to live in spirit, and have simply been transferred to a new realm to await resurrection. There is rejoicing in that knowledge.*

Answer: **2 Nephi 9:6**	Commentary:
6 For as death hath passed upon all men, to fulfil the merciful plan of the great Creator, there must needs be a power of resurrection, and the resurrection must needs come unto man by reason of the fall; and the fall came by reason of transgression; and because man became fallen they were cut off from the presence of the Lord.	*When someone dies, the sadness is that we miss them. The "good news" is that death is a part of the Plan of Happiness and returns us to our heavenly home. There will be a resurrection of the dead.* *Death is a part of living . . . and living in eternity is a part of death.*

Answer: **Alma 12:24**

Commentary:

24 And we see that death comes upon mankind, yea, the death which has been spoken of by Amulek, which is the temporal death; nevertheless there was a space granted unto man in which he might repent; therefore this life became a probationary state; a time to prepare to meet God; a time to prepare for that endless state which has been spoken of by us, which is after the resurrection of the dead.

"Life does not begin with birth, nor does it end with death. Prior to our birth, we dwelled as spirit children with our Heavenly Father. There we eagerly anticipated the possibility of coming to earth and obtaining a physical body. Knowingly we wanted the risks of mortality, which would allow the exercise of agency and accountability. But we regarded the returning home as the best part of that long-awaited trip, just as we do now. Before embarking on any journey, we like to have some assurance of a round-trip ticket. Returning from earth to a life in our heavenly home requires passage through—not around—the doors of death. We were born to die, and we die to live. As seedlings of God, we barely blossom on earth; we fully flower in heaven." (Russell M. Nelson, "Doors of Death," general conference, April 1992.)

Knowing that death is a part of the plan softens (if we will allow it) the deep pain and sorrow associated with it.

QUESTION 18

Is there a life after death? Why shouldn't I seek for all the pleasure I can in life?

Answer: **2 Nephi 1:14–15**	Commentary:
14 Awake! and arise from the dust, and hear the words of a trembling parent, whose limbs ye must soon lay down in the cold and silent grave, from whence no traveler can return; a few more days and I go the way of all the earth. 15 But behold, the Lord hath redeemed my soul from hell; I have beheld his glory, and I am encircled about eternally in the arms of his love.	*Lehi is pleading with his children to understand that he will pass through the portal of death very soon. He states that there is another life as he crosses the threshold into the loving arms of the Lord.* *Ecclesiastes 12:24 states, "Then shall the dust return to the earth as it was: and the spirit shall return unto God who gave it."* *The question, "Is there life after death?" is answered by many religions with a resounding "yes."*

Answer: **Helaman 13:38**	Commentary:
38 But behold, your days of probation are past; ye have procrastinated the day of your salvation until it is everlastingly too late, and your destruction is made sure; yea, for ye have sought all the days of your lives for that which ye could not obtain; and ye have sought for happiness in doing iniquity, which thing is contrary to the nature of that righteousness which is in our great and Eternal Head.	*We are on earth to be tested. There is life after death. Perhaps it is best to say, "There is life after life." How we live our lives here on earth determines much about the condition of our lives in the next life.* *We should understand that there are no long-term benefits for choosing only earthly pleasure. How we live here determines the conditions we will operate under in the next life. It does matter how we live now!*

Answer: **Mosiah 16:10–11**	Commentary:
10 Even this mortal shall put on immortality, and this corruption shall put on incorruption, and shall be brought to stand before the bar of God, to be judged of him according to their works whether they be good or whether they be evil— 11 If they be good, to the resurrection of endless life and happiness; and if they be evil, to the resurrection of endless damnation, being delivered up to the devil, who hath subjected them, which is damnation—	*We will die and be held accountable for our actions and choices while here on earth. We will face a judgment, and it will be determined if our works (actions) were worthy of blessings and rewards in the next life.* *"Hedonism" means "self-indulgence, pleasure-seeking, self-gratification, lotus-eating, sybaritism; intemperance, immoderation, extravagance, luxury, or high living."* *Concern for self is the exact opposite of Heavenly Father's instruction to His children.*

Answer: **3 Nephi 13:19–21**	Commentary:
19 Lay not up for yourselves treasures upon earth, where moth and rust doth corrupt, and thieves break through and steal;	*Jesus Christ's invitation is for us to be cautious about focusing upon temporal concerns, which can be stolen or ruined, versus that which has lasting value .*
20 But lay up for yourselves treasures in heaven, where neither moth nor rust doth corrupt, and where thieves do not break through nor steal.	*We do well to remember that we will take nothing with us except the relationships we've forged, the joy that comes from serving people, and the happiness we've obtained through knowing that we are in good standing with God.*
21 For where your treasure is, there will your heart be also.	

QUESTION 19

If there really is a God, why does He allow
so much suffering and injustice on the earth?

Answer: **Helaman 14:30**

30 And now remember, remember, my brethren, that whosoever perisheth, perisheth unto himself; and whosoever doeth iniquity, doeth it unto himself; for behold, ye are free; ye are permitted to act for yourselves; for behold, God hath given unto you a knowledge and he hath made you free.

Commentary:

Perhaps the question could be rephrased, "Since there is a God, why does He allow so much suffering and injustice on the earth?" Or turn the question around: "Why do we tend to assign the blame for suffering and injustice upon a Heavenly Father who loves us?"

Fundamental to Heavenly Father's plan is "agency" or "the power and the right to choose happiness by keeping His commandments, or captivity, which comes from sin." Therefore, He will never take away the agency of anyone. If we think about it, most suffering and injustice come from the exercise of agency by those who are focused on power, self-service, greed, intolerance, hatred, impatience, vice, pride, laziness, disobedience, or general godlessness. A significant amount of suffering and injustice finds fertile ground in governments, neighborhoods, and families, where people use their agency to choose evil over good.

War is caused by man, not by God. Poverty is often a result of someone exercising their agency to accumulate or to control wealth and resources. Murder and killing are generally godless attempts to take away the God-given agency of others. In summary, we should be very cautious about assigning blame to Heavenly Father. We must understand that there will be those who, using their agency—God's indispensible component of His purpose for us—sadly choose for themselves that which negatively effects others.

If God took away agency, He would be taking away a fundamental pillar of His Plan for us.

Answer: **Alma 32:6; 62:41**

6 And now when Alma heard this, he turned him about, his face immediately towards him, and he beheld with great joy; for he beheld that their afflictions had truly humbled them, and that they were in a preparation to hear the word.

Commentary:

Heavenly Father desires the growth and happiness of His children. Many times, suffering and challenge can be the precursor to preparing hearts and minds to receive Him and His will.

The Zoramites (who were apostate Nephites) were troubled by a severe class distinction. However, the poverty inflicted upon the poorer class truly produced a richness in their hearts, and they were ready to receive the gospel and come to Christ.

41 But behold, because of the exceedingly great length of the war between the Nephites and the Lamanites many had become hardened, because of the exceedingly great length of the war; and many were softened because of their afflictions, insomuch that they did humble themselves before God, even in the depth of humility.

The Nephites experienced severe afflictions caused by the ravages of a war that lasted for many years. The length and severity of the war actually helped many of them to see important contrasts—to see the emptiness that hostility and bloodshed produced. Their hearts were softened by their afflictions. By contrast, others were hardened because of their afflictions. God allowed the suffering and allowed His children to choose their response to it.

Many individuals or families have been blessed by seasons of difficulty (health challenges, job losses, bankruptcy, relationship woes, or situations that cause one to consider the need to turn to a greater power than themselves). It is often the case that those who have "hit bottom," those who are "down and out," or those who "have come to the end of their rope" are prepared and give way to an attitude that is ready to repent, change, and find God and Christ.

For those who turn to Him, Heavenly Father allows the greatest good to come from situations where affliction and difficulty abound. His desire is that we allow Him to carry our burdens—or make them light—while we orient ourselves to eternal priorities.

Answer: **Alma 14:11; 60:13**	Commentary:
11 But Alma said unto him: The Spirit constraineth me that I must not stretch forth mine hand; for behold the Lord receiveth them up unto himself, in glory; and he doth suffer that they may do this thing, or that the people may do this thing unto them, according to the hardness of their hearts, that the judgments which he shall exercise upon them in his wrath may be just; and the blood of the innocent shall stand as a witness against them, yea, and cry mightily against them at the last day.	*Sometimes the Lord allows the suffering and challenges that come as a result of others' inappropriate exercise of agency to serve as a witness in judgement against them.* *There is a God in Heaven. He is just. Affliction and suffering may be used to condemn the wicked. To those who have been distressed or damaged by the unrighteous actions of others, the Lord will give a righteous reward.*
13 For the Lord suffereth the righteous to be slain that his justice and judgment may come upon the wicked; therefore ye need not suppose that the righteous are lost because they are slain; but behold, they do enter into the rest of the Lord their God.	*It is important to remember that eternity is much longer than the relatively few decades we live here on earth. Choices and our response to our circumstances here in mortality do impact the state of affairs in eternities. Suffering and injustice may serve as judgement and witness for each of us as eternal justice is meted out by our just and fair Father in Heaven.*

Answer: **2 Nephi 2:24; 9:20**	Commentary:
24 But behold, all things have been done in the wisdom of him who knoweth all things.	*We do have a Heavenly Father who loves us! Forever we must remember that He knows all things. He is Holy. He will be just and utilize the events and circumstances in this life to the maximum collective benefit*

	of all of His children. Some will suffer and be blessed for it, and others will be condemned by their repeated choices to sin.
20 O how great the holiness of our God! For he knoweth all things, and there is not anything save he knows it.	We must trust Him.

Answer: **2 Nephi 2:1–2**	Commentary:
1 And now, Jacob, I speak unto you: Thou art my first-born in the days of my tribulation in the wilderness. And behold, in thy childhood thou hast suffered afflictions and much sorrow, because of the rudeness of thy brethren.	*Jacob began his life in very difficult circumstances related to hunger and other general challenges of living in the wilderness. Moreover, he was exposed to rude and obnoxious brothers who complained and made life difficult.*
2 Nevertheless, Jacob, my first-born in the wilderness, thou knowest the greatness of God; and he shall consecrate thine afflictions for thy gain.	*Heavenly Father understands all things. A promise is given to Jacob by his earthly father, Lehi, who was also a prophet. He tells Jacob that God can and will consecrate, or make holy, all the injustices and suffering experienced in our lives. These things will be devoted and set apart for our good.*

Answer: **Ether 12:6**	Commentary:
6 And now, I, Moroni, would speak somewhat concerning these things; I would show unto the world that faith is things which are hoped for and not seen; wherefore, dispute not because ye see not, for ye receive no witness until after the trial of your faith.	*Much of our experience is also used by Heavenly Father to check or give trial to our faith. The first principle of the gospel is faith. Our Heavenly Father, who loves us, will consecrate our experience for our good if we trust in His divine understanding.*

QUESTION 20
Why is baptism required for eternal salvation?

Answer: **2 Nephi 31:5**	Commentary:
5 And now, if the Lamb of God, he being holy, should have need to be baptized by water, to fulfil all righteousness, O then, how much more need have we, being unholy, to be baptized, yea, even by water!	*Nephi taught that even Christ, who was the only perfect person to ever live upon the earth, needed to obtain the ordinance of baptism by water. A person who has an advanced understanding of the body and its functions is not awarded a medical degree until all the requirements and credentials are met. A person born into a Spanish-speaking home who develops fluent Spanish language skills, is not given a college degree in Spanish until prescribed criteria are met and exams give evidence that a degree is merited. Perfection does not eliminate the need to receive the ordinance of baptism—a criterion set by the Lord.*

Answer: **Alma 7:14**	Commentary:
14 Now I say unto you that ye must repent, and be born again; for the Spirit saith if ye are not born again ye cannot inherit the kingdom of heaven; therefore come and be baptized unto repentance, that ye may be washed from your sins, that ye may have faith on the Lamb of God, who taketh away the sins of the world, who is mighty to save and to cleanse from all unrighteousness.	*Alma taught that faith in Christ and His Atonement is a critical preliminary to repentance and baptism. Further, he taught that without the formal ordinance of baptism, we cannot receive the informal but critical cleansing from our sins. Just as a baby is born in the flesh, we must all experience "being born again" as a witness that we desire our repentance to change us and qualify us for God's kingdom. As a newborn child takes on the surname of his parent, the symbolic new birth at baptism requires that we take upon ourselves the name of our heavenly savior—Christ. Instead of becoming a Jones, Gonzalez, or Schmidt, we become Christians and bear the name of Christ. We seek to live as He would. We would not want to do or say anything that would bring shame to the family name. This level of new commitment evidenced by the ordinance of baptism is essential for our salvation.*

Answer: **2 Nephi 31:17**	Commentary:
17 Wherefore, do the things which I have told you I have seen that your Lord and your Redeemer should do; for, for this cause have they been shown unto me, that ye might know the gate by which ye should enter. For the gate by which ye should enter is repentance and baptism by water; and then cometh a remission	*Christ sets the rules. We live by those rules in order to receive the reward. Nephi affirms that he knows that the requirement of baptism is requisite to receiving a remission of sins. He uses the metaphor of a gate and states without reservation or exception that both repentance and baptism by water are requirements for receiving a remission of sins.*

of your sins by fire and by the Holy Ghost.	*God has given the commandment that we enter the gate by following gospel principles. One of those commandments is to formalize our commitment to a new life by receiving the ordinance of baptism of water. This prepares us for the next commandment to receive and be cleansed by the Holy Ghost.*

QUESTION 21

Where was I before I was born?

Answer: **Alma 13:3**

3 And this is the manner after which they were ordained—being called and prepared from the foundation of the world according to the foreknowledge of God, on account of their exceeding faith and good works; in the first place being left to choose good or evil; therefore they having chosen good, and exercising exceedingly great faith, are called with a holy calling, yea, with that holy calling which was prepared with, and according to, a preparatory redemption for such.

Commentary:

Before we were born, we lived with Heavenly Father. We were given the agency to choose good over evil, exercise our faith, and prepare ourselves to come to earth.

Speaking to the young women of the church, Sister Elaine Dalton taught, "You are young women of great faith. You brought your faith with you when you came to the earth. Alma teaches us that in the premortal realms you exhibited 'exceeding faith and good works.' You fought with your faith and testimony to defend the plan that was presented by God. You knew the plan was good, and you knew that the Savior would do what He said He would do—because you knew Him! You stood with Him, and you were eager for your opportunity to come to earth. You knew what was going to be required of you. You knew it would be difficult, and yet you were confident not only that you could accomplish your divine mission but that you could make a difference. You are 'choice spirits' who were reserved to come forth in the fulness of times to take part in laying the foundations of the great latter-day work, including the building of the temples and the performance of ordinances therein."

We existed long before we came to earth, and we will continue to live after we pass from this mortal existence.

Answer: **Helaman 14:17**

17 But behold, the resurrection of Christ redeemeth mankind, yea, even all mankind, and bringeth them back into the presence of the Lord.

Commentary:

Helaman taught of Christ's role in redeeming mankind. He stated that we would be brought back to the presence of the Lord, which teaches us that we were there before we came to earth. We will go back to His presence.

Answer: **Alma 42:7–9**

7 And now, ye see by this that our first parents were cut off both temporally and spiritually from the presence of the Lord; and thus we see they became subjects to follow after their own will.

Commentary:

As Adam and Eve were in the presence of the Lord before the Fall, we can see how the Fall cut each of us off from the presence of the Lord. We were in His presence before the Fall, and because of the effects of the Atonement of Jesus Christ, we are reclaimed.

8 Now behold, it was not expedient that man should be reclaimed from this temporal death, for that would destroy the great plan of happiness.

9 Therefore, as the soul could never die, and the fall had brought upon all mankind a spiritual death as well as a temporal, that is, they were cut off from the presence of the Lord, it was expedient that mankind should be reclaimed from this spiritual death.

QUESTION 22

Does God really answer prayers?

Answer: **Mormon 9:21**	Commentary:
21 Behold, I say unto you that whoso believeth in Christ, doubting nothing, whatsoever he shall ask the Father in the name of Christ it shall be granted him; and this promise is unto all, even unto the ends of the earth.	*First notice the promise: "whatsoever he shall ask the Father in the name of Christ it shall be granted him." Then Moroni adds an exclamation by saying, "this promise is unto all, even unto the ends of the earth." If we really believe in His Son Jesus Christ and trust Him and His will, we will receive an answer to all prayers.*
	However, we are answered in ways that we do not always recognize at the moment. Perhaps the commentary about this scripture by Elder Richard G. Scott will assist in answering this question: "Help from the Lord generally comes in increments. . . . Not all our prayers will be answered as we wish. It is not always

easy to know the will of the Lord, yet there are some things we can be certain of. He will never ask us to do anything that is not completely in harmony with His teachings. Our earnest prayers are answered when they conform to the will of the Lord. Since we cannot perfectly understand His will, we must walk with faith. He is all-knowing, and His decisions are perfect. The fact that our finite capacity does not let us understand all of His dealings with man does not limit Him from blessing us. His will is our best choice in life, whether or not we fully understand it. When we act using our moral agency wisely, the Lord will act according to His will . . . We see such a limited part of the eternal plan He has fashioned for each one of us. Trust Him, even when in eternal perspective it temporarily hurts very much. Have patience when you are asked to wait when you want immediate action. He may ask you to do things which are powerfully against your will. Exercise faith and say, Let Thy will be done. Such experiences, honorably met, prepare you and condition you for yet greater blessings." ("Obtaining Help from the Lord," general conference, October 1991.)

Answer: **Mosiah 27:14**	Commentary:
14 And again, the angel said: Behold, the Lord hath heard the prayers of his people, and also the prayers of his servant, Alma, who is thy father; for he has prayed with much faith concerning thee that thou mightest be brought to the knowledge of the truth; therefore, for this purpose have I come to convince thee of the power and authority of God, that the prayers of his servants might be answered according to their faith.	*The Lord does hear the prayers of His people, and he answers them! With our finite understanding, it is difficult to understand the infinite capacity of our Father in Heaven. It is important that we pray with faith and trust.* *Just as God heard the humble prayer of a father pleading for his son, so does Heavenly Father hear and answer our prayers. Answers come most often in subtle, quiet ways that might not be in the way we expect. Prayers are often answered through the words and actions of others or perhaps in quiet, tender mercies that simply give to our troubled hearts confidence that He is mindful of us and our petitions.*

Answer: **Mosiah 9:18**	Commentary:
18 And God did hear our cries and did answer our prayers; and we did go forth in his might; yea, we did go forth against the Lamanites, and in one day and a night we did slay three thousand and forty-three; we did slay them even until we had driven them out of our land.	*Zeniff understood that prayers were not only heard, but also answered. However, he didn't stand still, waiting for the answer. Instead, he went forth and acted as if everything depended upon him. He went out and fought his battles against the enemy in a focused and heartfelt way. It was then that he saw the hand of God not only protecting him and his people, but also helping them in winning by expelling the enemy from their lands.* *Heavenly Father will truly answer the humble who sincerely ask and move forward in faith.*

Answer: **Mosiah 24:12–13, 19**

12 And Alma and his people did not raise their voices to the Lord their God, but did pour out their hearts to him; and he did know the thoughts of their hearts.

13 And it came to pass that the voice of the Lord came to them in their afflictions, saying: Lift up your heads and be of good comfort, for I know of the covenant which ye have made unto me; and I will covenant with my people and deliver them out of bondage

19 And in the morning the Lord caused a deep sleep to come upon the Lamanites, yea, and all their task-masters were in a profound sleep.

Commentary:

This is a wonderful story of answered prayer. God does answer even the silent, pleading prayers of the heart.

Amulon had been appointed jurisdiction over Alma and his humble colony of converts. Amulon and Alma were former colleagues in King Noah's court. We can see that Amulon desired to use his authority to severely hamper the Nephites in their new religious commitments, persecuting them (even to death) and not allowing them the privilege of personal or public prayer.

In this situation the people prayed in their hearts, and the Lord knew the thoughts of their silent prayers. He answered with a miracle that allowed them to escape from Lamanite bondage.

Answer: **Enos 1:1–5**

1 Behold, it came to pass that I, Enos, knowing my father that he was a just man—for he taught me in his language, and also in the nurture and admonition of the Lord—and blessed be the name of my God for it—

2 And I will tell you of the wrestle which I had before God, before I received a remission of my sins.

Commentary:

Enos had an experience wherein he received an answer to his prayer. It is important to note that his answer was preceded by a lot of preparation.

He began by considering his greatest earthly blessings. He felt something very special when he thought of his father. Just the thought of his dad made him feel grateful. Thoughts of gratitude and an acknowledgement of what God has already

3 Behold, I went to hunt beasts in the forests; and the words which I had often heard my father speak concerning eternal life, and the joy of the saints, sunk deep into my heart.

4 And my soul hungered; and I kneeled down before my Maker, and I cried unto him in mighty prayer and supplication for mine own soul; and all the day long did I cry unto him; yea, and when the night came I did still raise my voice high that it reached the heavens.

5 And there came a voice unto me, saying: Enos, thy sins are forgiven thee, and thou shalt be blessed.

given us is important as we seek for further blessings.

Enos sought the answer regarding his status in God's eyes. He wanted to be forgiven—to be pure before God.

He spent the entire day in an environment conducive to prayer and meditation. Whether he was in a kneeling position for an entire day or simply in an attitude of searching for his answer is not clear. We can see from the record that he first had a great desire and then took time to think in an environment where an answer could come.

Finally, after hours, the answer came.

We must do our part to consider our blessings and acknowledge his mercy toward us. We should put ourselves in circumstances and in an environment that allows us to ponder, pray, and contemplate—perhaps in nature as Enos did or in the Mountain of the Lord (His temple).

Perhaps the answers come in the quiet, early-morning hours in our home or as we ponder during the sacrament. We must remember that, while God does answer prayers, He does it on His timetable and not on ours. He desires that we pay a price and learn lessons along the way. He may answer in minutes or it might take hours, days, or even years. His only purpose in withholding answers might be that He knows important lessons will be learned along the way in our forests of yearning.

QUESTION 23
Why is God so soft-spoken most of the time?

Answer: **Alma 37:6–7**	Commentary:
	Perhaps another way of asking the question is, "How does He answer our prayers?"
6 Now ye may suppose that this is foolishness in me; but behold I say unto you, that by small and simple things are great things brought to pass; and small means in many instances doth confound the wise.	*The Lord might at times be very soft-spoken. In fact, He often answers our prayers through the written words of God and His holy prophets.*
	One important principle taught by this scripture is the all important fact that big results from our prayers often are brought about by "small and simple things."
7 And the Lord God doth work by means to bring about his great and eternal purposes; and by very small means the Lord doth confound the wise and bringeth about the salvation of many souls.	*Many times we might be looking for big or dramatic answers to our prayers, and all the while there is a simple key found in some seemingly small and simple verse of scripture.*

Answer: **1 Nephi 10:19**	Commentary:
19 For he that diligently seeketh shall find; and the mysteries of God shall be unfolded unto them, by the power of the Holy Ghost, as well in these times as in times of old, and as well in times of old as in times to come; wherefore, the course of the Lord is one eternal round.	*It is important to remember that God communicates His answers through the third member of the Godhead, The Holy Ghost. Seldom does Heavenly Father answer our prayers in a sensational manner. There truly is a quietness about the stirrings and nudgings—answers—that come to us through the Holy Ghost.*
2 Nephi 32:5	*The Holy Ghost "shows." He doesn't shout. The word "show" means "to cause to be visible, make known, or reveal." Those actions are most often quiet in nature. The sunrise each day shows or reveals the landscape very slowly and quietly as darkness is replaced with light. Often answers to prayer come in the same way.*
5 For behold, again I say unto you that if ye will enter in by the way, and receive the Holy Ghost, it will show unto you all things what ye should do.	

Answer: **1 Nephi 17:45**	Commentary:
45 Ye are swift to do iniquity but slow to remember the Lord your God. Ye have seen an angel, and he spake unto you; yea, ye have heard his voice from time to time; and he hath spoken unto you in a still small voice, but ye were past feeling, that ye could not feel his words; wherefore, he has spoken unto you like unto the voice of thunder, which did cause the earth to shake as if it were to divide asunder.	*Laman and Lemuel are examples of those who can have many manifestations that were the opposite of soft-spoken, and yet they never really understood. Loud and obvious answers won't make much sense to those who are not in-tune or prepared. Answers come to inquiring humble hearts—not necessarily to a demanding murmurer or cynic. In the end, if we seek answers we must still qualify and atune ourselves to be ready to hear the "still, small voice."*

Answer: **Alma 5:45–46**	Commentary:
45 And this is not all. Do ye not suppose that I know of these things myself? Behold, I testify unto you that I do know that these things whereof I have spoken are true. And how do ye suppose that I know of their surety? 46 Behold, I say unto you they are made known unto me by the Holy Spirit of God. Behold, I have fasted and prayed many days that I might know these things of myself. And now I do know of myself that they are true; for the Lord God hath made them manifest unto me by his Holy Spirit; and this is the spirit of revelation which is in me.	*Alma teaches us that just asking for answers is generally not enough. He points out that he did more than just ask and then carry out the work. He hastened or accelerated the process of receiving his desired answer by coupling inquiry with a sacrifice to put himself in a condition to understand the Lord's answer.* *The Holy Spirit is the means for receiving spiritual promptings or quiet answers. Therefore, it is important to atune ourselves to that channel. However, we should also remember that answers come to prepared and humble hearts while they are moving their feet in action, and not when they are hid up in the quiet chamber of some dark closet waiting for it.*

Answer: **Alma 12:9–10**	Commentary:
9 And now Alma began to expound these things unto him, saying: It is given unto many to know the mysteries of God; nevertheless they are laid under a strict command that they shall not impart only according to the portion of his word which he doth grant unto the children of men, according to the heed and diligence which they give unto him.	*To "give heed" means to "pay attention to, take notice of, take note of, pay heed to, attend to, listen to, bear in mind, be mindful of, mind, mark, consider, take into account, follow, obey, adhere to, abide by, observe, take to heart, or be alert to."* *To be "diligent" means to be characterized by "conscientiousness, hard work, application, concentration, effort, care, industriousness, rigor, meticulousness, thoroughness, perseverance, persistence, tenacity, dedication, commitment, or tirelessness."*

10 And therefore, he that will harden his heart, the same receiveth the lesser portion of the word; and he that will not harden his heart, to him is given the greater portion of the word, until it is given unto him to know the mysteries of God until he know them in full.

Through diligent heeding, we qualify to be given more understanding of those things the Lord wants to impart. As always, those things will be given in a quiet, soft, and sometimes inaudible manner. It's possible the Lord has already given us the answer, but we didn't hear it.

Elder Richard G. Scott taught in October 1989 general conference the following: "If you feel that God has not answered your prayers . . . then carefully look for evidence in your own life of His having already answered you."

To help each of us recognize answers given, the Lord said: "If you desire a further witness, cast your mind upon the night that you cried unto me in your heart, that you might know concerning the truth of these things.

"Did I not speak peace to your mind concerning the matter?" D&C 6:22–23.

God's soft voice through the Holy Ghost has often already spoken, but we have missed it. Think back, and you might find He's already spoken.

QUESTION 24

Why do I need Christ, and not just His teachings, to be happy?

Answer: **Alma 36**
(the whole chapter with emphasis on the following verses:)

13 Yea, I did remember all my sins and iniquities, for which I was tormented with the pains of hell; yea, I saw that I had rebelled against my God, and that I had not kept his holy commandments.

14 Yea, and I had murdered many of his children, or rather led them away unto destruction; yea, and in fine so great had been my iniquities, that the very thought of coming into the presence of my God did rack my soul with inexpressible horror.

Commentary:

In this chapter, Alma the Younger is recounting the story of his conversion. His past included not only persecuting the church and bringing pain to his father who was the prophet, but also, because of his power to influence others, leading many others away from God.

He described the moment when he felt that he wished he could become extinct or just go away. When he understood whom he had been, what he had done, and the impact of those actions upon his eternal life, he just wanted to "not be."

15 Oh, thought I, that I could be banished and become extinct both soul and body, that I might not be brought to stand in the presence of my God, to be judged of my deeds.	*This pain and agony extended over a period of three days and three nights. As Alma continued in pain, he remembered something his father had taught: The coming of Jesus Christ, the Son of God, to atone for the sins of the world.*
16 And now, for three days and for three nights was I racked, even with the pains of a damned soul.	*To "atone" means to "make amends for, make reparation for, make restitution for, make up for, compensate for, pay for, recompense for, expiate, redress, make good, offset, or do penance for."*
17 And it came to pass that as I was thus racked with torment, while I was harrowed up by the memory of my many sins, behold, I remembered also to have heard my father prophesy unto the people concerning the coming of one Jesus Christ, a Son of God, to atone for the sins of the world.	*That thought brought Alma hope that perhaps there was a solution to his anguish.* *Christ is the greatest teacher who ever lived. He taught great things, and he was a model without fault. However, He is much more! He is our Savior and Redeemer. To have eternal happiness, we must have a redeemer who atones for, makes restitution for, repairs, and makes amends for our imperfect ways.*

Answer: **2 Nephi 25:23, 25–26**	Commentary:
23 For we labor diligently to write, to persuade our children, and also our brethren, to believe in Christ, and to be reconciled to God; for we know that it is by grace that we are saved, after all we can do.	*Jesus Christ taught principles through parables and stories which, if heeded and applied, will make our lives happier.* *His role in the Great Plan of Happiness designed by our Heavenly Father is much greater than just "teacher" and "example." We are sinners and we are imperfect.*

	He is sinless and perfect. He lived, died, and then broke the bands or permanency of death by being resurrected. His role as Savior and Redeemer permits us to be perfected and to also live again.
25 For, for this end was the law given; wherefore the law hath become dead unto us, and we are made alive in Christ because of our faith; yet we keep the law because of the commandments.	
	We cannot do any of that on our own. Yes, we can live a good life and be ethical in our dealings with our fellow man. We can serve others and be kind. We can do many things of our own free will to bless those around us. However, we cannot resurrect ourselves or pay for our own sins, except by repentance and giving our sins to Christ.
26 And we talk of Christ, we rejoice in Christ, we preach of Christ, we prophesy of Christ, and we write according to our prophecies, that our children may know to what source they may look for a remission of their sins.	
	Christ is our source for redemption from both physical death and spiritual death.

Answer: **Alma 34:15**	Commentary:
15 And thus he shall bring salvation to all those who shall believe on his name; this being the intent of this last sacrifice, to bring about the bowels of mercy, which overpowereth justice, and bringeth about means unto men that they may have faith unto repentance.	Bringing salvation to all mankind is the role of a savior. Through His mercy and personal sacrifice for each one of us, He brings to us the possibility of not getting what we deserve as sinners.
	He has paid the price of sin, conditional upon our faith in Him and our repentant desire to change from our natural ways.

Answer: **2 Nephi 31:20-21**

20 Wherefore, ye must press forward with a steadfastness in Christ, having a perfect brightness of hope, and a love of God and of all men. Wherefore, if ye shall press forward, feasting upon the word of Christ, and endure to the end, behold, thus saith the Father: Ye shall have eternal life.

21 And now, behold, my beloved brethren, this is the way; and there is none other way nor name given under heaven whereby man can be saved in the kingdom of God. And now, behold, this is the doctrine of Christ, and the only and true doctrine of the Father, and of the Son, and of the Holy Ghost, which is one God, without end. Amen.

Commentary:

The doctrine of Christ is fundamental to Heavenly Father's Great Plan of Happiness. Jesus paid for our sins and promises to forgive us, on the condition that we accept Him by exercising our faith in Him, repenting, receiving baptism by immersion, receiving the gift of the Holy Ghost, and striving faithfully to keep His commandments all the days of our lives. However, we should remember that in paying for our sins, Christ did not eliminate our responsibility to live in accordance with His requirements.

There is no other way to receive salvation without Jesus Christ.

QUESTION 25

What does Jesus Christ expect of me, and what is my part?

Answer: **3 Nephi 12:48, 27:27**	Commentary:
48 Therefore I would that ye should be perfect even as I, or your Father who is in heaven is perfect.	*Christ himself explained the level of effort that we as disciples should exert in what He expects of us. He stated that our objective should be to become like Him and our Heavenly Father. That's a tall order, and impossible without them.*
27 And know ye that ye shall be judges of this people, according to the judgment which I shall give unto you, which shall be just. Therefore, what manner of men ought ye to be? Verily I say unto you, even as I am. (also see Matt. 5:48 to see His same instruction in the Bible)	*"Perfection," as defined by the dictionary, is interesting. Included in the definition is the following: "pursuit of being as free as possible from all flaws or defects." Continuing, it states, "the action or process of improving something until it is as faultless as possible." The thesaurus gives words like "improvement, betterment, refinement, refining, and honing."*

	The Lord expects us to "discipline" ourselves and therefore be "disciples" forever, seeking to improve and become as faultless as possible. We should seek to emulate Him and become refined in His attributes.

Answer: **Alma 34:32**	Commentary:
32 For behold, this life is the time for men to prepare to meet God; yea, behold the day of this life is the day for men to perform their labors.	*Heavenly Father has given us a period of years in mortality to prepare to meet Him. He expects us to learn to conduct ourselves as Christians. He expects us to labor, toil, work, sweat, struggle, and become more like Him by keeping His commandments and accepting Christ as our Savior and Redeemer.*

Answer: **Mosiah 2:17**	Commentary:
17 And behold, I tell you these things that ye may learn wisdom; that ye may learn that when ye are in the service of your fellow beings ye are only in the service of your God.	*Jesus Christ expects us to learn to serve one another. This means we not only need to serve and love others, but also allow ourselves to be served and loved. We become like God when we are outside of ourselves in selfless giving.*

Answer: **Moroni 7:46–48**	Commentary:
46 Wherefore, my beloved brethren, if ye have not charity, ye are nothing, for charity never faileth. Wherefore, cleave unto charity,	*Jesus Christ expects us to understand that all commandments revolve around the condition of the heart—charity.*

which is the greatest of all, for all things must fail—

47 But charity is the pure love of Christ, and it endureth forever; and whoso is found possessed of it at the last day, it shall be well with him.

48 Wherefore, my beloved brethren, pray unto the Father with all the energy of heart, that ye may be filled with this love, which he hath bestowed upon all who are true followers of his Son, Jesus Christ; that ye may become the sons of God; that when he shall appear we shall be like him, for we shall see him as he is; that we may have this hope; that we may be purified even as he is pure. Amen.

He is clear in His instruction that charity is the greatest of all attributes and that we must strive to develop it. All other attributes fail without the cardinal attribute of His pure love. He invites us to "pray unto the Father with all the energy of heart" to develop and be filled with charity. If we seek to become like Him, we must emulate this highest form of love.

Answer: **Moroni 7:44–45**

Commentary:

44 If so, his faith and hope is vain, for none is acceptable before God, save the meek and lowly in heart; and if a man be meek and lowly in heart, and confesses by the power of the Holy Ghost that Jesus is the Christ, he must needs have charity; for if he have not charity he is nothing; wherefore he must needs have charity.

45 And charity suffereth long, and is kind, and envieth not, and is not puffed up, seeketh not her own, is

Charity is incorporated into other attributes that we are expected to develop while here on earth.

We are to suffer long or develop "longsuffering," becoming patient, forgiving, and understanding. We are to avoid envy, jealousy, covetousness, and discontent. We are to check our pride and be less focused on the self. He asks us not to become easily provoked or aroused to anger. He expects us to steer clear of any kind of evil and to live with righteous focus. We are expected to take delight in truth and

not easily provoked, thinketh no evil, and rejoiceth not in iniquity but rejoiceth in the truth, beareth all things, believeth all things, hopeth all things, endureth all things.	*truthfulness, to be submissive to Heavenly Father's will by bearing our burdens with trust while maintaining hope that all will turn out well.* *He expects us to try to become like Him.*

Answer: **2 Nephi 9** (the entire chapter, with emphasis on verse 41) 41 O then, my beloved brethren, come unto the Lord, the Holy One. Remember that his paths are righteous. Behold, the way for man is narrow, but it lieth in a straight course before him, and the keeper of the gate is the Holy One of Israel; and he employeth no servant there; and there is none other way save it be by the gate; for he cannot be deceived, for the Lord God is his name.	Commentary: *Christ expects us to come unto Him. He clearly reminds us that His way is straight and narrow. His path is not easy, but through it we can have eternal life.* *Our part is to accept and to follow Him and His way.*

QUESTION 26
Why do we need a living prophet?

Answer: **Mosiah 8:7–18**

7 And the king said unto him: Being grieved for the afflictions of my people, I caused that forty and three of my people should take a journey into the wilderness, that thereby they might find the land of Zarahemla, that we might appeal unto our brethren to deliver us out of bondage.

8 And they were lost in the wilderness for the space of many days, yet they were diligent, and found not the land of Zarahemla but returned to this land, having traveled in a land among many waters, having discovered a land which was covered with bones of men, and of beasts, and was also covered with

Commentary:

Background and context: King Limhi was leader over the Nephite colony in the Land of Nephi when Mosiah (king of the main group of Nephites living in Zarahemla) assigned a Mulekite man named Ammon to go on an expedition. His objective was to find the lost Nephite colony that had departed Zarahemla three generations earlier.

When Ammon and his search party of fifteen men found the colony, they were under Lamanite bondage. Limhi and his people had lost their understanding of the need for prophets. They had also become spiritually disoriented under the prideful rule of Limhi's father, King Noah, who

ruins of buildings of every kind, having discovered a land which had been peopled with a people who were as numerous as the hosts of Israel.

9 And for a testimony that the things that they had said are true they have brought twenty-four plates which are filled with engravings, and they are of pure gold.

10 And behold, also, they have brought breastplates, which are large, and they are of brass and of copper, and are perfectly sound.

11 And again, they have brought swords, the hilts thereof have perished, and the blades thereof were cankered with rust; and there is no one in the land that is able to interpret the language or the engravings that are on the plates. Therefore I said unto thee: Canst thou translate?

14 And behold, the king of the people who are in the land of Zarahemla is the man that is commanded to do these things, and who has this high gift from God.

15 And the king said that a seer is greater than a prophet.

16 And Ammon said that a seer is a revelator and a prophet also; and

had ordered the burning of the Prophet Abinadi. Consequently, King Noah later was burned at the stake by his own army.

Sometime earlier, Limhi had sent a search party looking for Zarahemla—potentially to get aid from them to assist in getting out from under Lamanite bondage. While they had no success in finding Zarahemla, they did discover ruins of a previous civilization, the Jaredites. As evidence, they collected bones, rusty swords, shields, and other instruments of war. Among their findings they discovered a record written on gold plates. However, they couldn't decipher the language.

When Ammon and his search party arrived and discovered the lost colony, Limhi and his people were delighted. But they were also confused regarding the identity of the ruins and people whose civilization they had discovered on their search expedition. King Limhi inquired if Ammon knew of anyone who could translate the records engraved on plates.

Ammon's reply gives us a wonderful response to the question, "Why do we need a living prophet?"

He responded that, yes, there existed such a man—their prophet and king, Mosiah. He added additional insight in teaching Limhi of the doctrine of prophets, who are also seers and revelators.

Read carefully verses 15–17. Let the scriptural text of Ammon's reply speak to you

a gift which is greater can no man have, except he should possess the power of God, which no man can; yet a man may have great power given him from God.

17 But a seer can know of things which are past, and also of things which are to come, and by them shall all things be revealed, or, rather, shall secret things be made manifest, and hidden things shall come to light, and things which are not known shall be made known by them, and also things shall be made known by them which otherwise could not be known.

18 Thus God has provided a means that man, through faith, might work mighty miracles; therefore he be cometh a great benefit to his fellow beings.

about prophets, seers, and revelators.

We need prophets, seers, and revelators who can orient us by remembering events and teachings from the past, help us by seeing things we need to know for the present, and guide us by their understanding of the future.

Our loving Father in Heaven gives us prophets, and has always done so, to the end that they can be of great benefit to us.

The Heavens are not closed. We have latter-day prophets (Apostles) presided over by the Prophet.

Answer: **3 Nephi 1:13**

Commentary:

13 Lift up your head and be of good cheer; for behold, the time is at hand, and on this night shall the sign be given, and on the morrow come I into the world, to show unto the world that I will fulfil all that which I have caused to be spoken by the mouth of my holy prophets.

Just prior to the birth of the Savior in the old world, a Nephite prophet by the name of Nephi helped the people to understand the signs associated with the advent of the Son of God. His birth had been prophesied by all prior prophets. Without a prophet in the Americas, the people could not know the significance of a strange, bright, new star. With a prophet, they were taught truth and new anticipations important to their spiritual welfare.

Answer: **Mosiah 3:13**	Commentary:
13 And the Lord God hath sent his holy prophets among all the children of men, to declare these things to every kindred, nation, and tongue, that thereby whosoever should believe that Christ should come, the same might receive remission of their sins, and rejoice with exceedingly great joy, even as though he had already come among them.	*One role of prophets through the ages of time is to help us believe in Christ. They help us to understand His role and Atonement.*

Answer: **1 Nephi 10:4**	Commentary:
4 Yea, even six hundred years from the time that my father left Jerusalem, a prophet would the Lord God raise up among the Jews —even a Messiah, or, in other words, a Savior of the world.	*Lehi, a prophet, gave critical insight to his family that God would raise up a Messiah, even His Son, to be the Savior of the world.* *We need prophets to orient us.*

Answer: **2 Nephi 3:14–16, 18, 20**	Commentary:
14 And thus prophesied Joseph, saying: Behold, that seer will the Lord bless; and they that seek to destroy him shall be confounded; for this promise, which I have obtained of the Lord, of the fruit of my loins, shall be fulfilled. Behold, I am sure of the fulfilling of this promise;	*Prophets quote prophets. They help us to understand the meaning of prophesies from the past.* *Here Lehi explains the relationship between Joseph of Egypt and a future prophet to bear the same name, who would also bear the name of his father.*

15 And his name shall be called after me; and it shall be after the name of his father. And he shall be like unto me; for the thing, which the Lord shall bring forth by his hand, by the power of the Lord shall bring my people unto salvation.

16 Yea, thus prophesied Joseph: I am sure of this thing, even as I am sure of the promise of Moses; for the Lord hath said unto me, I will preserve thy seed forever.

Joseph of Egypt prophesied. Lehi affirms it.

18 And the Lord said unto me also: I will raise up unto the fruit of thy loins; and I will make for him a spokesman. And I, behold, I will give unto him that he shall write the writing of the fruit of thy loins, unto the fruit of thy loins; and the spokesman of thy loins shall declare it.

Then Joseph of Egypt indicates that this new prophet Joseph will also bring forth the writings of the descendants of Joseph of Egypt.

Those writings will come from the dust to people of a future time.

20 And they shall cry from the dust; yea, even repentance unto their brethren, even after many generations have gone by them. And it shall come to pass that their cry shall go, even according to the simpleness of their words.

Prophets orient and help us to make connections and to understand more clearly.

Answer: **Jacob 4:4, 6**	Commentary:
4 For, for this intent have we written these things, that they may know that we knew of Christ, and we had a hope of his glory many hundred years before his coming; and not only we ourselves had a hope of his glory, but also all the holy prophets which were before us.	*Prophets testify of Christ and help us to understand His purpose as Savior and Redeemer.*
6 Wherefore, we search the prophets, and we have many revelations and the spirit of prophecy; and having all these witnesses we obtain a hope, and our faith becometh unshaken, insomuch that we truly can command in the name of Jesus and the very trees obey us, or the mountains, or the waves of the sea.	*We search the teachings and revelations of the prophets to give us hope in Christ, and also to know that prophets act in the name of Jesus Christ in doing marvelous things.*

Answer: **1 Nephi 22:2**	Commentary:
2 And I, Nephi, said unto them: Behold they were manifest unto the prophet by the voice of the Spirit; for by the Spirit are all things made known unto the prophets, which shall come upon the children of men according to the flesh.	*The voice of the Spirit makes all things known unto the prophets. Listening to them will assist us in directing our lives wisely.*

Answer: **Helaman 5:18**	Commentary:
18 And it came to pass that Nephi and Lehi did preach unto the Lamanites with such great power and authority, for they had power and authority given unto them that they might speak, and they also had what they should speak given unto them—	*Prophets are given the power and authority to speak and communicate the will of Heavenly Father*

Answer: **Mosiah 4:30**	Commentary:
30 But this much I can tell you, that if ye do not watch yourselves, and your thoughts, and your words, and your deeds, and observe the commandments of God, and continue in the faith of what ye have heard concerning the coming of our Lord, even unto the end of your lives, ye must perish. And now, O man, remember, and perish not.	*Benjamin, a prophet and king, concluded his lengthy sermon to his people by giving them an admonition with this simple counsel.*
	We need prophets to remind, encourage, warn, and bless us. The intent of prophets is to protect us from perishing in the war against Satan.

QUESTION 27

How can I know God's will for me?

Answer: **2 Nephi 32:8–9**

8 And now, my beloved brethren, I perceive that ye ponder still in your hearts; and it grieveth me that I must speak concerning this thing. For if ye would hearken unto the Spirit which teacheth a man to pray, ye would know that ye must pray; for the evil spirit teacheth not a man to pray, but teacheth him that he must not pray.

9 But behold, I say unto you that ye must pray always, and not faint; that ye must not perform any thing unto the Lord save in the first place ye shall pray unto the Father in the name of Christ, that he will

Commentary:

At times it seems very difficult to know what Heavenly Father wants us to do or what His will is for us. He invites us to pray. He also warns us that Lucifer does not want us to connect to heaven through prayer and will do all he can to discourage us from doing so.

Nephi reminds us that if we want to understand God's will for us, we must pray always and not falter or become distant from His influence.

Nephi then provides us with wonderful counsel regarding what we should pray for. We cannot be paralyzed by inaction when we are wondering about God's will for us. Nephi directs us to pray that

consecrate thy performance unto thee, that thy performance may be for the welfare of thy soul.	*Heavenly Father will consecrate our actions for the welfare of our souls. Instead of just wishing for guidance, we should pray according to our best judgement, asking the Lord to consecrate or make holy our steps.*

Answer: **Words of Mormon 1:7**	Commentary:
7 And I do this for a wise purpose; for thus it whispereth me, according to the workings of the Spirit of the Lord which is in me. And now, I do not know all things; but the Lord knoweth all things which are to come; wherefore, he worketh in me to do according to his will.	*Heavenly Father speaks to man through the whisperings of the Spirit. He knows all things, and everything will work according to His will.* *Maintaining our connection with the Lord will help us take the steps we need to take, even though most often we won't know how things will work out. We know that He knows, so we trust Him and His will.*

Answer: **2 Nephi 32:3**	Commentary:
3 Angels speak by the power of the Holy Ghost; wherefore, they speak the words of Christ. Wherefore, I said unto you, feast upon the words of Christ; for behold, the words of Christ will tell you all things what ye should do.	*Elder Scott once said, "If you want to speak to God, then pray. If you want God to speak to you, read the scriptures." Great counsel! Should you go on a mission? Read the scriptures! Should you make a certain investment? Read the scriptures! Want to know God's will for you? Read the scriptures!*

154

Answer: **2 Nephi 10:24–25**	Commentary:
23 Therefore, cheer up your hearts, and remember that ye are free to act for yourselves—to choose the way of everlasting death or the way of eternal life.	*We must remember that agency and the power to choose are ours. If we want to know God's will for us, we must first reconcile ourselves to Him and those things that He has commanded us.*
24 Wherefore, my beloved brethren, reconcile yourselves to the will of God, and not to the will of the devil and the flesh; and remember, after ye are reconciled unto God, that it is only in and through the grace of God that ye are saved.	*"To reconcile" means, "to be compatible, in harmony, united, and yoked together."* *When we have that trust, we are free to make our own choices, remembering that He will sustain and bless us "according to His will."*

Answer: **Mosiah 23:21–22**	Commentary:
21 Nevertheless the Lord seeth fit to chasten his people; yea, he trieth their patience and their faith. 22 Nevertheless—whosoever putteth his trust in him the same shall be lifted up at the last day. Yea, and thus it was with this people.	*Sometimes we might prayerfully choose, yet things don't work out. Or perhaps we just plain make a poor decision. If our hearts are right, the Lord will chasten or purify us with a trial of our patience and faith. If we put our trust in Him and continue to do our best, we will win in the end.*

Answer: **Ether 2:21–22; 3:1–5**	Commentary:
21 And it came to pass that the brother of Jared did so, according as the Lord had commanded. 22 And he cried again unto the Lord saying: O Lord, behold I have	*Background and context: The brother of Jared had built barges in accordance to the commandment and direction of the Lord. He had a concern that he shared with the Lord regarding air to breathe*

done even as thou hast commanded me; and I have prepared the vessels for my people, and behold there is no light in them. Behold, O Lord, wilt thou suffer that we shall cross this great water in darkness?

23 And the Lord said unto the brother of Jared: What will ye that I should do that ye may have light in your vessels? For behold, ye cannot have windows, for they will be dashed in pieces; neither shall ye take fire with you, for ye shall not go by the light of fire.

1 And it came to pass that the brother of Jared, (now the number of the vessels which had been prepared was eight) went forth unto the mount, which they called the mount Shelem, because of its exceeding height, and did molten out of a rock sixteen small stones; and they were white and clear, even as transparent glass; and he did carry them in his hands upon the top of the mount, and cried again unto the Lord, saying:

2 O Lord, thou hast said that we must be encompassed about by the floods. Now behold, O Lord, and do not be angry with thy servant because of his weakness before thee; for we know that thou art holy and dwellest in the heavens, and that we are bunworthy before thee; because of the fall our natures have become evil continually; neverthe-

inside the vessels and light so they would not have to travel in darkness.

The Lord directed him in how to resolve the first problem of oxygen to breathe. Then He reviewed the solutions for light that would not work and asked the brother of Jared for his thoughts.

The brother of Jared then went to work to find a solution. He exerted great effort and brainpower to execute a plan—to melt ore and create from that ore sixteen clear stones. By any standard, that was a significant effort.

He took the stones to the mount.

The brother of Jared then approached the Lord in prayer. He rehearsed the Lord's commandment to pray and to call upon the Lord in their time of need, that they would receive according to desires.

less, O Lord, thou hast given us a commandment that we must call upon thee, that from thee we may receive according to our desires.

3 Behold, O Lord, thou hast smitten us because of our iniquity, and hast driven us forth, and for these many years we have been in the wilderness; nevertheless, thou hast been merciful unto us. O Lord, look upon me in pity, and turn away thine anger from this thy people, and suffer not that they shall go forth across this raging deep in darkness; but behold these things which I have molten out of the rock.

He then pleads for the Lord to understand their desire to travel in the raging deep waters with light—not darkness.

4 And I know, O Lord, that thou hast all power, and can do whatsoever thou wilt for the benefit of man; therefore touch these stones, O Lord, with thy finger, and prepare them that they may shine forth in darkness; and they shall shine forth unto us in the vessels which we have prepared, that we may have light while we shall cross the sea.

Placing the stones in front of himself, he pleads with the Lord, acknowledging the Lord's power to do anything for the benefit of man. In simpler terms, he both pleads for and understands God's power. In essence He says, "I've done a lot to prepare these stones. It was very labor intensive. Lord, will you touch my doings with your finger and make them shine light for us?" The Lord then touched the stones.

5 Behold, O Lord, thou canst do this. We know that thou art able to show forth great power, which looks small unto the understanding of men.

Many times we might be directed, stirred, moved, and shown the Lord's will for us. Most times we might only know of our desires. We must sometimes act and resolve problems in our weakness, then ask the Lord to "touch our doings."

Trusting His power, we accept His will in either blessing our efforts or changing our course.

QUESTION 28

How can I better teach others about the gospel?

Answer: **Alma 1:3**	Commentary:
3 But this is not all; they had given themselves to much prayer, and fasting; therefore they had the spirit of prophecy, and the spirit of revelation, and when they taught, they taught with power and authority of God.	*These young missionaries obtained the word of God and then gave themselves to much prayer and fasting. This assisted them in teaching with "power and authority."*

Answer: **2 Nephi 33:1**	Commentary:
1 And now I, Nephi, cannot write all the things which were taught among my people; neither am I mighty in writing, like unto speaking; for when a man speaketh by the power	*We must acknowledge and remember that we aren't the real teachers; the real teacher is the Holy Ghost. With that understanding, we put our emphasis on qualifying for the Holy Ghost through*

of the Holy Ghost the power of the Holy Ghost carrieth it unto the hearts of the children of men.	*obedience and willingness to submit to the real teacher.*

Answer: **Jacob 1:7**	Commentary:
7 Wherefore we labored diligently among our people, that we might persuade them to come unto Christ, and partake of the goodness of God, that they might enter into his rest, lest by any means he should swear in his wrath they should not enter in, as in the provocation in the days of temptation while the children of Israel were in the wilderness.	*We remember that the purpose of our teaching is to persuade and bring others to Christ and to partake of the goodness of God. The focus must not be on us, our goodness, or our style of teaching. The sole purpose of our teaching and message is to bring others to Christ.*

Answer: **1 Nephi 19:23**	Commentary:
23 And I did read many things unto them which were written in the books of Moses; but that I might more fully persuade them to believe in the Lord their Redeemer I did read unto them that which was written by the prophet Isaiah; for I did liken all scriptures unto us, that it might be for our profit and learning.	*Using the scriptures and likening them unto those we teach will enhance our capacity to teach with power. The words of the scriptures are the words of God. The Holy Ghost is commissioned to testify of truth. When we use scripture, the real teacher teaches.*

Answer: **2 Nephi 4:15–16**	Commentary:
15 And upon these I write the things of my soul, and many of the scriptures which are engraven upon the plates of brass. For my soul delighteth in the scriptures, and	*As we study and delight in the scriptures by pondering and learning from them, our understanding and capacity to teach from them is increased. Learning and studying*

my heart pondereth them, and writeth them for the learning and the profit of my children. 16 Behold, my soul delighteth in the things of the Lord; and my heart pondereth continually upon the things which I have seen and heard.	*scripture will make us more powerful in teaching others about the gospel.*

Answer: **Alma 13:23**	Commentary:
23 And they are made known unto us in plain terms, that we may understand, that we cannot err;	*Learning to teach in plain terms, according to the understanding of those we teach, and helping them to understand so they cannot err, will help us teach with power.*

QUESTION 29
What should I do when the goals I set require a significant change in direction?

Answer: **Alma 56** (the entire chapter, with emphasis on the following verses)

6 And now ye also know concerning the covenant which their fathers made, that they would not take up their weapons of war against their brethren to shed blood.

7 But in the twenty and sixth year, when they saw our afflictions and our tribulations for them, they were about to break the covenant which they had made and take up their weapons of war in our defence.

8 But I would not suffer them that they should break this covenant which they had made, supposing

Commentary:

This is a great story to answer this question of the soul. Life sometimes seems to get in the way of our goals. We research, ponder, consider, survey, study, and then make a judgement about which direction we should go in life. A goal is set. We begin a calculated strategy to execute that goal, and then an obstacle or new situation arises that requires a significant change in direction. We sometimes feel frustrated either with the shifting sands of change, with our own inability to have seen the new variable coming, or in not making a contingency plan. This story helps us to see that things change—not only on the battlefield, but also in the trenches of life! New shifts require modified campaigns

that God would strengthen us, insomuch that we should not suffer more because of the fulfilling the oath which they had taken.

and sometimes wholesale revamping of our goals and strategies.

The converts from the missionary efforts of the four sons of Mosiah were so focused upon the change that had occurred in their lives that they made a covenant never to return to their past sin of shedding blood in war. A covenant was something significant to them. They no doubt taught their children to follow in that covenant.

However, the challenges associated with the Nephites' defending their liberties resulted in war as a part of the landscape for many years. Since the sons of those converts had neither taken the oath nor made covenants, it was finally determined that they could assist in the war. Because of their inexperience and youth, they were assigned responsibilities other than hand-to-hand combat.

9 But behold, here is one thing in which we may have great joy. For behold, in the twenty and sixth year, I, Helaman, did march at the head of these two thousand young men to the city of Judea, to assist Antipus, whom ye had appointed a leader over the people of that part of the land.

10 And I did join my two thousand sons, (for they are worthy to be called sons) to the army of Antipus, in which strength Antipus did rejoice exceedingly; for behold, his army had been reduced by the Lamanites because their forces had slain a vast number of our men, for which cause we have to mourn.

A strategy or goal was not to have the sons of these converts engage in warfare or the shedding of blood. A plan was formulated. These young men would serve as decoys. They would pretend to be delivering provisions and supplies to the Nephite cities.

30 Now when we saw that the Lamanites began to grow uneasy on this wise, we were desirous to bring a stratagem into effect upon them; therefore Antipus ordered that I should march forth with my

Military leaders conferred and determined that the young men should take their course near the city of Antiparah as if they were carrying supplies. The hope of this action was to entice the Lamanite

little sons to a neighboring city, as if we were carrying provisions to a neighboring city.

army to follow them, and then to diffuse the Lamanites' strength.

31 And we were to march near the city of Antiparah, as if we were going to the city beyond, in the borders by the seashore.

Plans were made, goals were set, an execution scheme was devised, and preliminary marching orders were given.

32 And it came to pass that we did march forth, as if with our pro visions, to go to that city.

33 And it came to pass that Antipus did march forth with a part of his army, leaving the remainder to maintain the city. But he did not march forth until I had gone forth with my little army, and came near the city Antiparah.

The goal was to distract and pull the strongest army of the Lamanites away from the city. Meanwhile, the seasoned Nephite army positioned itself to retake the city of Antiparah and ultimately defeat the Lamanite stronghold. And Helaman's young men would move out of the battle zone and not have to fight.

34 And now, in the city Antiparah were stationed the strongest army of the Lamanites; yea, the most numerous.

As the "supply train" made its way near the city of Antiparah, the execution of their goal to decoy and distract the Lamanite armies worked!

35 And it came to pass that when they had been informed by their spies, they came forth with their army and marched against us.

The strategy was brilliant, and it appeared as though the implementation was flawless.

36 And it came to pass that we did flee before them, northward. And thus we did lead away the most powerful army of the Lamanites;

37 Yea, even to a considerable distance, insomuch that when they saw the army of Antipus pursuing them, with their might, they did not turn to the right nor to the left, but pursued their march in a straight course after us; and, as we suppose, it was their intent to slay us before Antipus should overtake them, and this that they might not be surrounded by our people.

38 And now Antipus, beholding our danger, did speed the march of his army. But behold, it was night; therefore they did not overtake us, neither did Antipus overtake them; therefore we did camp for the night.

39 And it came to pass that before the dawn of the morning, behold, the Lamanites were pursuing us. Now we were not sufficiently strong to contend with them; yea, I would not suffer that my little sons should fall into their hands; therefore we did continue our march, and we took our march into the wilderness.

40 Now they durst not turn to the right nor to the left lest they should be surrounded; neither would I turn to the right nor to the left lest they should overtake me, and we could not stand against them, but be slain, and they would make their escape; and thus we did flee all that day into the wilderness, even until it was dark.

Then things started to change. The Lamanite armies went after the decoy supply train with the intent to not only cut off the provisions going to the Nephites, but also slay the young men of the caravan.

Antipus (the Nephite Army general) therefore had to do a double-time run to catch up with the Lamanite army and engage them in battle so they would not annihilate the inexperienced young men of Helaman. Human reason suggested that any Lamanite engagement of those untrained and amateur decoys would be easy pickings.

Though they fled through the night, just before dawn Helaman's young men were about to fall into the hands of the Lamanite army. The young men, no doubt overcome by fear, hastily fled again.

41 And it came to pass that again, when the light of the morning came we saw the Lamanites upon us, and we did flee before them.

Then the Lamanite army paused! Helaman and his decoy supply train of 2,000 young men were left to wonder why they had stopped pursuing them.

42 But it came to pass that they did not pursue us far before they halted; and it was in the morning of the third day of the seventh month.

43 And now, whether they were overtaken by Antipus we knew not, but I said unto my men: Behold, we know not but they have halted for the purpose that we should come against them, that they might catch us in their snare;

Helaman supposed that either Antipus (the Nephite general) and his army had finally overtaken them from the rear and were now fighting, or the Lamanite army was baiting Helaman's sons to come back and be caught in a sure death trap.

Because of the speed of travel required by Antipus to overtake the Lamanites, they were sure to be tired and not ready for battle.

44 Therefore what say ye, my sons, will ye go against them to battle?

45 And now I say unto you, my beloved brother Moroni, that never had I seen so great courage, nay, not amongst all the Nephites.

Helaman posed a question to the young men: Should they continue out of harm's way or turn back and see if the travel-worn Nephite soldiers needed support?

46 For as I had ever called them my sons (for they were all of them very young) even so they said unto me: Father, behold our God is with us, and he will not suffer that we should fall; then let us go forth; we would not slay our brethren if they would let us alone; therefore let us go, lest they should overpower the army of Antipus.

The boys indicated a desire to help, even though they had no battle experience and had grown up without any mind-set of war.

47 Now they never had fought, yet they did not fear death; and they did think more upon the liberty of their fathers than they did upon their lives; yea, they had been taught by their mothers, that if they did not doubt, God would deliver them.

48 And they rehearsed unto me the words of their mothers, saying: We do not doubt our mothers knew it.

49 And it came to pass that I did return with my two thousand against these Lamanites who had pursued us. And now behold, the armies of Antipus had overtaken them, and a terrible battle had commenced.

50 The army of Antipus being weary, because of their long march in so short a space of time, were about to fall into the hands of the Lamanites; and had I not returned with my two thousand they would have obtained their purpose.

51 For Antipus had fallen by the sword, and many of his leaders, because of their weariness, which was occasioned by the speed of their march—therefore the men of Antipus, being confused because of the fall of their leaders, began to give way before the Lamanites.

As the record states, they did return, and their assistance was a critical element in winning the battle.

They credited their mothers for teaching them to trust in God.

The battle was terrible. It was obvious that, had Helaman and his young men not returned, the conflict would have favored the strong Lamanite army, leaving the Nephites weakened, killed, or captured.

The entire war could have taken a turn for a significant Lamanite advantage. Instead, the victory positioned the Nephites for ultimate conquest.

Goals, along with their tactical procedures, do shift and change in the battles of life. All well-designed strategies can require modification when situations change. One might have a perfect blueprint for a delightful ending in a career, a church calling, or a family endeavor— only to find that a health issue, an untimely death, or an economic downturn changes everything.

52 And it came to pass that the Lamanites took courage, and began to pursue them; and thus were the Lamanites pursuing them with great vigor when Helaman came upon their rear with his two thousand, and began to slay them exceedingly, insomuch that the whole army of the Lamanites halted and turned upon Helaman.

53 Now when the people of Anti pus saw that the Lamanites had turned them about, they gathered together their men and came again upon the rear of the Lamanites.

54 And now it came to pass that we, the people of Nephi, the people of Antipus, and I with my two thou sand, did surround the Lamanites, and did slay them; yea, insomuch that they were compelled to deliver up their weapons of war and also themselves as prisoners of war.

56 But behold, to my great joy, there had not one soul of them fal len to the earth; yea, and they had fought as if with the strength of God; yea, never were men known to have fought with such miraculous strength; and with such mighty power did they fall upon the Lamanites, that they did frighten them; and for this cause did the Lamanites deliver themselves up as prisoners of war.

The Lamanite converts had entered into a covenant not to fight or shed blood, and they would have taught their children the same ideal. Though covenants are never negotiable, those who had not taken an oath had to rethink and change their direction in the matter of war.

The Nephite military leaders had carefully designed goals that had to be changed when the elements of the battle changed. Helaman did not desire to plunge his young decoy team into what seemed would be certain death. But the situation changed and so did the need. Helaman had to alter his preferences in favor of meeting the needs of others.

And so it goes. We might chart well-crafted paths to certain destinations in life—the perfect education, career, marriage, family, or political ambition. However, there might enter into the tactical equation an unforeseen element that causes us to reevaluate and reexamine values, to the end that we change our goals and formulate new plans.

As we do so, the Lord, in His goodness, will consecrate our changes to a course that blesses us in ways we could not have seen when we were required to modify our goals.

Helaman was astonished to realize that "not one soul" of his 2,000 sons had fallen. Though many were wounded in his little army, the miracle of survival attested to the faith and trust of these extraordinary sons.

QUESTION 30

How serious is abortion, and what can I say to someone investigating the Church who has had one or more?

It is important to understand that the order of the Church and Lord in matters such as abortion is to always include the wisdom, counsel, and judgement of inspired priesthood leaders. It is unwise to give personal opinion or to make statements about whether unwise and short-sighted decisions of the past are justified. Leave the responsibility to judge to those authorized to do so.

Answer: **Mosiah 13:21**	Commentary:
21 Thou shalt not kill.	*The Lord is rather direct and clear, isn't He? In Doctrine and Covenants 59:6, He adds other clarifying language: "nor anything like unto it." By any divine standard, killing or taking the life of another is a serious sin.*
	As for forgiveness of this sin, it is good to note the commentary and counsel of Elder Russell M. Nelson. The conference address in its entirety is an excellent resource. Note these few words from the talk:
	"Now, is there hope for those who have so sinned without full understanding, who now suffer heartbreak? Yes. So far as is known, the Lord does not regard this

transgression as murder. And 'as far as has been revealed, a person may repent and be forgiven for the sin of abortion.' Gratefully, we know the Lord will help all who are truly repentant.

Yes, life is precious! No one can cuddle a cherished newborn baby, look into those beautiful eyes, feel the little fingers, and caress that miraculous creation without deepening reverence for life and for our Creator.

Life comes from life. It is a gift from our Heavenly Father. It is eternal, as he is eternal. Innocent life is not sent by Him to be destroyed! This doctrine is not of me, but is that of the living God and of His divine Son, which I testify in the name of Jesus Christ, amen." ("Reverence for Life," Russell M. Nelson, general conference, April 1985.)

Answer: **3 Nephi 12:21**	Commentary:
21 Ye have heard that it hath been said by them of old time, and it is also written before you, that thou shalt not kill, and whosoever shall kill shall be in danger of the judgment of God;	*Taking life has always been a sin. Anyone who does so will be judged. Since agency is central to Heavenly Father's Plan, anyone who eliminates it through taking life is in danger of significant or harsh judgement. Participating in an abortion in any way allows the accountable to inflict or take away the agency of the innocent.*

Answer: **Alma 9:13**	Commentary:
13 Behold, do ye not remember the words which he spake unto Lehi, saying that: Inasmuch as ye shall keep my commandments, ye shall prosper in the land? And again it is said that: Inasmuch as ye will not keep my commandments ye shall be cut off from the presence of the Lord.	*Keeping commandments brings prosperity and the good will of God. We are always blessed when we keep the commandments. However, not keeping the commandments causes us to be cut off from the influence of God (particularly the third member of the Godhead—the Holy Ghost). Ultimately, we cannot be in the presence of God unless we demonstrate by our actions that we keep the commandments and value His counsel.*

Answer: **Alma 14:11**	Commentary:
11 But Alma said unto him: The Spirit constraineth me that I must not stretch forth mine hand; for behold the Lord receiveth them up unto himself, in glory; and he doth suffer that they may do this thing, or that the people may do this thing unto them, according to the hardness of their hearts, that the judgments which he shall exercise upon them in his wrath may be just; and the blood of the innocent shall stand as a witness against them, yea, and cry mightily against them at the last day.	*Alma and Amulek were subjected to observing women and children being burned and consumed in the fire. Alma taught that those innocent would be received up unto glory. However, their blood would stand as a witness against those who made conscious choices to violate the commandments of God.*

QUESTION 31

Can I repent of my sins and really be forgiven?

Answer: **Mosiah 26:30–32**	Commentary:
30 Yea, and as often as my people repent will I forgive them their trespasses against me.	*Heavenly Father loves us! Understanding that we all sin, He made it possible for us to repent and be forgiven. If we are honestly trying to change, there are no restrictions regarding how many times we can repent and be forgiven.*
31 And ye shall also forgive one another your trespasses; for verily I say unto you, he that forgiveth not his neighbor's trespasses when he says that he repents, the same hath brought himself under condemnation.	*Since God is willing to forgive us countless times, He expects us to do as He does—to forgive others with that same attitude. It appears that forgiveness for our sins depends upon our willingness to forgive others. "Condemnation" is a heavy word that means "to censure, disapprove, or rebuke."*
32 Now I say unto you, Go; and whosoever will not repent of his sins the same shall not be numbered	*Repentance, or change, is requisite for us to be forgiven and included in Heavenly Father's kingdom. Forgiveness shall be*

among my people; and this shall be observed from this time forward.	*extended to all who repent with the motive of keeping His commandments.*

Answer: **Alma 5:33**	Commentary:
33 Behold, he sendeth an invitation unto all men, for the arms of mercy are extended towards them, and he saith: Repent, and I will receive you.	*The phrase "arms of mercy" is duly descript. Heavenly Father remains open-armed with the love and desire to receive any of His children who are willing to repent and do His will. He reaches out with His very long arms as He invites us to make course corrections when we've erred.*

Answer: **Alma 32:13–14**	Commentary:
13 And now, because ye are compelled to be humble blessed are ye; for a man sometimes, if he is compelled to be humble, seeketh repentance; and now surely, whosoever repenteth shall find mercy; and he that findeth mercy and endureth to the end the same shall be saved. 14 And now, as I said unto you, that because ye were compelled to be humble ye were blessed, do ye not suppose that they are more blessed who truly humble themselves because of the word?	*Humility is a key to repentance and to being forgiven. It is best for us to choose to be humble by seeking the will of Christ. But because He loves us, the Lord allows our experiences to humble us so that we will repent.* *The word "humble" means to be "modest, selfless, free of pride, common, unpretentious, and without actions showing an inflated view of self or rank."* *The word "seek" means "to ask for, solicit, call for, beg for, petition for, appeal for, apply for."* *If we are humble, and we seek to repent, the Lord will extend mercy, leniency, compassion, kindness, and forgiveness. It is His desire to do so!*

Answer: **Enos 1:2–8**	Commentary:
2 And I will tell you of the wrestle which I had before God, before I received a remission of my sins.	*Can we repent of our sins and really be forgiven? That largely depends upon our attitude. We must wrestle or wage a war against sin and lack of righteous focus.*
3 Behold, I went to hunt beasts in the forests; and the words which I had often heard my father speak concerning eternal life, and the joy of the saints, sunk deep into my heart.	*We must be "hungry" for a new life. Our prayers must be earnest with the desire to change. Sometimes we must pray for hours. We might find that the frequency, length, and quality of our prayer life needs to be increased.*
4 And my soul hungered; and I kneeled down before my Maker, and I cried unto him in mighty prayer and supplication for mine own soul; and all the day long did I cry unto him; yea, and when the night came I did still raise my voice high that it reached the heavens.	*Enos prayed all day and into the night. He struggled, wrestled, and fought to feel the connection between himself and God. This battle required more than a faint-hearted Christian. He desired to feel the peace that comes from a remission of sins.*
5 And there came a voice unto me, saying: Enos, thy sins are forgiven thee, and thou shalt be blessed.	*Finally a voice came unto him, and he felt the calm assurance that he had been blessed by the Lord to know that his sins were forgiven. All guilt was swept away. Peace replaced self worry and concern over his status with God.*
6 And I, Enos, knew that God could not lie; wherefore, my guilt was swept away.	*He wanted to understand how such a flood of tranquility could be accomplished. The Lord explained in certain and simple terms: faith in Christ.*
7 And I said: Lord, how is it done?	
8 And he said unto me: Because of thy faith in Christ, whom thou hast never before heard nor seen. And many years pass away before he	*Thus it is with each of us. When we focus our attention on connecting with Heavenly Father through prayer and on increasing our faith in the Savior and Redeemer of the world, we experience a cancellation or remission of our sins. Our faith in*

shall manifest himself in the flesh; wherefore, go to, thy faith hath made thee whole.	*Christ makes us whole again. For Enos then, and for us now.*

Answer: **Moroni 6:8**	Commentary:
8 But as oft as they repented and sought forgiveness, with real intent, they were forgiven.	*Forgiveness can come when one begins to yearn for an answer. "Can I really be forgiven for the dumb and short-sighted choices I've made?" The answer is yes! Moroni, after wandering alone for thirty to forty years, gives a simple and uncomplicated answer. He states that not only can we be forgiven of our sins, but also we are given as many chances as we need to make the change in our lives and become "new" creatures in Christ.*

Answer: **Alma 12:33**	Commentary:
33 But God did call on men, in the name of his Son, (this being the plan of redemption which was laid) saying: If ye will repent, and harden not your hearts, then will I have mercy upon you, through mine Only Begotten Son;	*Since Heavenly Father's Plan is to rescue us from our sins, He calls upon all of us to be saved! However, we have to take the step and respond with action. When we do our part, He reciprocates with mercy and forgives us.* *Therefore, receiving forgiveness depends on us and whether or not we will repent with full faith in Jesus Christ.*

Answer: **Mosiah 27:27–29**	Commentary:
27 I say unto you, unless this be the case, they must be cast off; and this I know, because I was like to be cast off.	*Alma the Younger, the four sons of Mosiah, and their friends were given a wake-up call from their sinful ways.*
28 Nevertheless, after wading through much tribulation, repenting nigh unto death, the Lord in mercy hath seen fit to snatch me out of an everlasting burning, and I am born of God.	*Alma explained his particular experience of being so sinful that he was nearly cast off. He explains, however, that the Lord was full of mercy and "snatched" him out of a demise of his own making.* *He was born of God. He was delivered from his miserable state and given a new chance to turn himself over to the Lord.*
29 My soul hath been redeemed from the gall of bitterness and bonds of iniquity. I was in the darkest abyss; but now I behold the marvelous light of God. My soul was racked with eternal torment; but I am snatched, and my soul is pained no more.	*He repented and was forgiven. With forgiveness came liberation from the pains he had experienced.*

Answer: **Alma 36:15–20, 24**	Commentary:
15 Oh, thought I, that I could be banished and become extinct both soul and body, that I might not be brought to stand in the presence of my God, to be judged of my deeds.	*Alma the Younger and his associates, the sons of Mosiah, were considered "the very vilest of all sinners" (Mosiah 28:4). In the process of his conversion, he felt as though he would rather die, vanish, or cease to exist rather than meet and be judged by the all-knowing God.*
16 And now, for three days and for three nights was I racked, even with the pains of a damned soul.	*He was racked with pain and felt as though he had no chance in this life or in the eternities. While in this state of torment and worry concerning his many*

17 And it came to pass that as I was thus racked with torment, while I was harrowed up by the memory of my many sins, behold, I remembered also to have heard my father prophesy unto the people concerning the coming of one Jesus Christ, a Son of God, to atone for the sins of the world.

personal sins, he remembered something else. He recalled having heard his father prophetically predict "the coming of one Jesus Christ, a Son of God, to atone for the sins of the world".

As he focused on that thought, he felt hope in Christ—that somehow, someway, there was a solution to his dead-end situation.

18 Now, as my mind caught hold upon this thought, I cried within my heart: O Jesus, thou Son of God, have mercy on me, who am in the gall of bitterness, and am encircled about by the everlasting chains of death.

Acting on that hope by repenting of his sins eventually brought forgiveness. His sins were remembered by God no more, and this once vile and offensive sinner became one of the great leaders for good in the Book of Mormon.

He repented and was forgiven. We can be too! Though we all sin, we can all be forgiven by allowing the Atonement to have full sway in our lives.

19 And now, behold, when I thought this, I could remember my pains no more; yea, I was harrowed up by the memory of my sins no more.

20 And oh, what joy, and what marvelous light I did behold; yea, my soul was filled with joy as exceeding as was my pain!

There is one important footnote to the issue of forgiveness when we repent. As we repent and are forgiven, can we really have our past deeds overridden and nullified? Though one may change themselves, what about the damage they've perpetuated upon other lives while in the sinful state of their past? Can anyone ever really

24 Yea, and from that time even until now, I have labored without ceasing, that I might bring souls unto repentance; that I might bring them to taste of the exceeding joy of which I did taste; that they might also be born of God, and be filled with the Holy Ghost.	*undo the consequences of their sin?* *In verse 24, Alma recognizes that while he can't undo the consequences upon others caused by the misdeeds in his past, he can live out the balance of his life trying to help others repent of their sins and taste of the joy he tasted in being forgiven. Much of our forgiveness comes in time as we help others to repent or to avoid the consequences of our past mistakes.*

Answer: **Mosiah 26:29–30** 29 Therefore I say unto you, Go; and whosoever transgresseth against me, him shall ye judge according to the sins which he has committed; and if he confess his sins before thee and me, and repenteth in the sincerity of his heart, him shall ye forgive, and I will forgive him also. 30 Yea, and as often as my people repent will I forgive them their trespasses against me.	*Commentary:* *The Lord is merciful. He will forgive those who come to Him in sincerity of heart and repentance. He does, however, require that the forgiven also be merciful and without bias—as He is. He requires us to forgive others. He states with clarity that He will forgive others as often as they repent. He requires that we do the same of our trespassers.* *He clarifies: "Wherefore, I say unto you, that ye ought to forgive one another; for he that forgiveth not his brother his trespasses standeth condemned before the Lord; for there remaineth in him the greater sin.* *"I, the Lord, will forgive whom I will forgive, but of you it is required to forgive all men" (Doctrine and Covenants 68:9–10).*

QUESTION 32

How can I balance between honestly searching for answers to doctrinal questions and delving into mysteries?

Answer: **Alma 40:1–3**	Commentary:
1 Now my son, here is somewhat more I would say unto thee; for I perceive that thy mind is worried concerning the resurrection of the dead.	It has been said that Heavenly Father's greatest joy and grief is found in His children. The same is true with earthly fathers and mothers and their children.
	Corianton was the cause of both joy and grief felt by his father, Alma the Younger. Corianton had committed sexual sin while in missionary service, which was no doubt a great source of sorrow for his earthly parents as well as his Heavenly Father.
2 Behold, I say unto you, that there is no resurrection—or, I would say, in other words, that this mortal does not put on immortality, this corruption does not put on in corruption—until after the coming of Christ.	But Alma identified another concern. Nearly one hundred years before the birth, crucifixion, and resurrection of the Savior, Corianton was worried and preoccupied over the mystery of the resurrection. It's one thing to be interested in

3 Behold, he bringeth to pass the resurrection of the dead. But behold, my son, the resurrection is not yet. Now, I unfold unto you a mystery; nevertheless, there are many mysteries which are kept, that no one knoweth them save God himself. But I show unto you one thing which I have inquired diligently of God that I might know—that is concerning the resurrection.

4 Behold, there is a time appointed that all shall come forth from the dead. Now when this time cometh no one knows; but God knoweth the time which is appointed.

5 Now, whether there shall be one time, or a second time, or a third time, that men shall come forth from the dead, it mattereth not; for God knoweth all these things; and it sufficeth me to know that this is the case—that there is a time appointed that all shall rise from the dead.

understanding doctrine, and another to be filled with unhealthy preoccupation. Corianton wanted to know details about a subject and event that was a century away. He wanted to know timetables and details.

Alma first taught Corianton what was known about the resurrection. Then he followed with counsel about the mystery of this event yet to be. "There are many mysteries which are kept, that no one knoweth save God himself." He said, "I have inquired too." In other words, it's not bad to wonder about the details of a certain doctrine. However, there is a point when we must be willing to be satisfied with what we have been given.

Alma gives classic counsel, which I paraphrase, "Son, here is what I do know. There is going to be a resurrection. I don't know the details, but God does. I am not sure if there is going to be a second resurrection, or a third or more. It doesn't matter—because God knows these things. There will be a resurrection, and there is a time appointed for it. That's good enough for me."

Alma didn't discourage seeking. However, he taught that there comes a time when we leave the details to God and move forward in our lives with what we do know.

QUESTION 33

What does God expect of me regarding the monetary success or financial woes of His children?

Answer: **Jacob 2:12–20**	Commentary:
12 And now behold, my brethren, this is the word which I declare unto you, that many of you have begun to search for gold, and for silver, and for all manner of precious ores, in the which this land, which is a land of promise unto you and to your seed, doth abound most plentifully.	*The question of money and its effect upon the heart has been something the Lord has given counsel about in the Book of Mormon and all Holy Writ. It seems to be less about quantity and more about its impact upon the heart and one's attitude.*
	While at the temple, Jacob taught priesthood holders about the challenge of personal economic success. He stated with some reproach that they had begun to search for wealth. It is interesting that the word "search" means "hunt for, look high and low for, ferret around for, rummage for, explore, scour, sift, quest, or turn inside out and leave no stone unturned." In other words, the Nephites had begun to

13 And the hand of providence hath smiled upon you most pleasingly, that you have obtained many riches; and because some of you have obtained more abundantly than that of your brethren ye are lifted up in the pride of your hearts, and wear stiff necks and high heads because of the costliness of your apparel, and persecute your brethren because ye suppose that ye are better than they.

14 And now, my brethren, do ye suppose that God justifieth you in this thing? Behold, I say unto you, Nay. But he condemneth you, and if ye persist in these things his judgments must speedily come unto you.

15 O that he would show you that he can pierce you, and with one glance of his eye he can smite you to the dust!

16 O that he would rid you from this iniquity and abomination. And, O that ye would listen unto the word of his commands, and let not this pride of your hearts destroy your souls!

turn their hearts to an unhealthy preoccupation with the acquisition of wealth or riches.

Jacob reminded them that divine intervention and God's will had blessed them—some more abundantly than others. The disparity of some having more than others had created a noxious condition of the heart—the sin of comparison. Class distinction then caused the universal sin of pride to creep into their hearts through the costliness of their external trappings and accessories (clothing).

The clothes weren't the problem; nor was it the fact that some had more money than others. But the differences transferred into the hearts of the people. They treated each other differently and dealt with one another based on the standard of possessions.

Jacob informed the people that the Lord was not happy with the hardening of their hearts. He called upon them to rid themselves of iniquity ("lack of righteous focus").

Riches and money are good. They bless, build, and support. However, preoccupation with money and possessions is that which destroys the soul. How many marriages have crumbled over the abundance or lack of money? How many civil or criminal lawsuits have been filed over misuse of perceived riches? How many business-related legal proceedings have been prosecuted over financial disputes?

How many family feuds have festered over the distribution of money left behind after the death of a loved one? Money, substance, and things without use of righteous focus destroys hearts and souls!

17 Think of your brethren like unto yourselves, and be familiar with all and free with your substance, that they may be rich like unto you.

Jacob then counsels the Nephites to freely give of their substance. He invites them to allow their success to bless those around them.

18 But before ye seek for riches, seek ye for the kingdom of God.

Keep first things first! Seek God and His kingdom!

Center yourself on Christ!

19 And after ye have obtained a hope in Christ ye shall obtain riches, if ye seek them; and ye will seek them for the intent to do good—to clothe the naked, and to feed the hungry, and to liberate the captive, and administer relief to the sick and the afflicted.

Then if you obtain riches, wonderful! However, seek them to the end that you can bless, clothe, feed, liberate, and administer relief to those who have greater need.

20 And now, my brethren, I have spoken unto you concerning pride; and those of you which have afflicted your neighbor, and persecuted him because ye were proud in your hearts, of the things which God hath given you, what say ye of it?

The matter of pride is a very personal one. It is completely and totally inappropriate for us to judge one another in this manner. Heavenly Father knows the condition of the heart. He knows where we are on the matter of pride, our attachment to things, and whether or not we have crossed inappropriate lines regarding our success or lack of it. The moment one starts to judge another, he is guilty of the same sin of pride. Best to self-examine and course correct as needed.

Answer: **3 Nephi 13:19–21**	Commentary:
19 Lay not up for yourselves treasures upon earth, where moth and rust doth corrupt, and thieves break through and steal;	*The Savior Himself counseled to be cautious about focusing too much on treasures that get old, rust, and that can easily walk away with the next villain.*
20 But lay up for yourselves treasures in heaven, where neither moth nor rust doth corrupt, and where thieves do not break through nor steal.	*Place Christ and heavenly treasures at the focus of your time and energy.* *Nowhere does He say that riches are bad. He just teaches us to keep our hearts focused on the things that matter long-term.*
21 For where your treasure is, there will your heart be also.	*It can be spiritually fatal to have hearts attached to treasures.*

Answer: **4 Nephi 1:3, 7, 16–18**	Commentary:
3 And they had all things common among them; therefore there were not rich and poor, bond and free, but they were all made free, and partakers of the heavenly gift.	*Fourth Nephi is a great endorsement of what happens when saints understand the importance of riches and don't allow prosperity to change hearts.*
7 And the Lord did prosper them exceedingly in the land; yea, insomuch that they did build cities again where there had been cities burned.	*The people were free with their success and consecrated their riches to lifting others. They experienced perhaps the longest stretch of financial prosperity the earth has ever seen—nearly 200 years.*
16 And there were no envyings, nor strifes, nor tumults, nor whoredoms, nor lyings, nor murders, nor any manner of lasciviousness; and surely there could not be a happier people among all the people who had been created by the hand of God.	*They had hearts free of pride and a natural focus on God and His Son Jesus Christ. They kept the commandments and avoided spiritual decline, which normally accompanies widespread prosperity. This state of affairs produced the happiest people ever created by God.*

17 There were no robbers, nor murderers, neither were there Lamanites, nor any manner of -ites; but they were in one, the children of Christ, and heirs to the kingdom of God.

18 And how blessed were they! For the Lord did bless them in all their doings; yea, even they were blessed and prospered.

They had created Zion—one mind and one heart. There were no haves and have nots. They weren't divided by politics or skin color or economic status. They were all Christians in the truest sense of the word.

This condition might not be able to be replicated universally at this time. However, we each can examine our own hearts and learn where we can adjust and find ways to apply the principles taught.

QUESTION 34

We live in a world where we are often asked to compromise or "sell out" on the beliefs and principles we hold dear. Is it okay to compromise to keep peace?

Answer: **Alma 11:1–3, 20–25**	Commentary:
1 Now it was in the law of Mosiah that every man who was a judge of the law, or those who were appointed to be judges, should receive wages according to the time which they labored to judge those who were brought before them to be judged.	*Mormon explains the wages or billings of judges. There are several verses that focus on monetary remuneration for legal services.*
2 Now if a man owed another, and he would not pay that which he did owe, he was complained of to the judge; and the judge executed authority, and sent forth officers that the man should be brought before him; and he judged the man according to the law and the evidences which were brought against him, and thus the man was	*We are oriented to the legal processes associated with litigation and judgement.*

compelled to pay that which he owed, or be stripped, or be cast out from among the people as a thief and a robber.

3 And the judge received for his wages according to his time—a senine of gold for a day, or a senum of silver, which is equal to a senine of gold; and this is according to the law which was given.

The discussion of money and payment for legal services sets us up for an impactful story. The verses in between highlight the monetary values.

20 Now, it was for the sole purpose to get gain, because they received their wages according to their employ, therefore, they did stir up the people to riotings, and all manner of disturbances and wickedness, that they might have more employ, that they might get money according to the suits which were brought before them; therefore they did stir up the people against Alma and Amulek.

21 And this Zeezrom began to question Amulek, saying: Will ye answer me a few questions which I shall ask you? Now Zeezrom was a man who was expert in the devices of the devil, that he might destroy that which was good; therefore, he said unto Amulek: Will ye answer the questions which I shall put unto you?

Zeezrom was one of the best in his profession (lawyer) and was determined to destroy anything good that came from Amulek.

22 And Amulek said unto him: Yea, if it be according to the Spirit of the Lord, which is in me; for

Zeezrom confidently made an offer of money (likely an extraordinary amount) to Amulek if he would deny his testimony of God.

I shall say nothing which is contrary to the Spirit of the Lord. And Zeezrom said unto him: Behold, here are six onties of silver, and all these will I give thee if thou wilt deny the existence of a Supreme Being.

23 Now Amulek said: O thou child of hell, why tempt ye me? Knowest thou that the righteous yieldeth to no such temptations?

Amulek answered with confidence, as if to say, "Do you think my testimony has a price?" or, "Do you really think you can get me to 'sell out' on my testimony for any amount of money?

24 Believest thou that there is no God? I say unto you, Nay, thou knowest that there is a God, but thou lovest that lucre more than him.

"There is not any amount of money that will 'buy' my testimony or cause me to deny what I know!"

What is our price? Will we sell out on our blessings, knowledge, ordinances, and so on for money?

25 And now thou hast lied before God unto me. Thou saidst unto me— Behold these six onties, which are of great worth, I will give unto thee— when thou hadst it in thy heart to retain them from me; and it was only thy desire that I should deny the true and living God, that thou mightest have cause to destroy me. And now behold, for this great evil thou shalt have thy reward.

Will we sell out for anything?

Not me!

QUESTION 35

As a mom, how can I best help my family at this time?

Answer: **Alma 56:44–48**

44 Therefore what say ye, my sons, will ye go against them to battle?

45 And now I say unto you, my beloved brother Moroni, that never had I seen so great courage, nay, not amongst all the Nephites.

46 For as I had ever called them my sons (for they were all of them very young) even so they said unto me: Father, behold our God is with us, and he will not suffer that we should fall; then let us go forth; we would not slay our brethren if they would let us alone; therefore let us go, lest they should overpower the army of Antipus.

Commentary:

The answer to this question is a very personal one. It is one that must be taken to the Lord in prayer. Sometimes there's no other option. Many times there is. In any case, this is a personal matter that must be studied carefully.

In this scripture block, Helaman discussed how impressed he was with the courage and almost unbelievable loyalty of 2,060 young Lamanite men who had never fought a single battle in their lives and had watched their convert parents (who had made a covenant to never fight) stay true to the promise they had made.

Helaman was stirred with astonishment and inspired by the level of goodness of

47 Now they never had fought, yet they did not fear death; and they did think more upon the liberty of their fathers than they did upon their lives; yea, they had been taught by their mothers, that if they did not doubt, God would deliver them.	*these young men who were selflessly willing to engage in battle against seasoned warriors.* *Helaman noted that the most impressive characteristic of these young men was that they had complete and total trust in God. They attributed their faith to the teachings and examples of their mothers.*
48 And they rehearsed unto me the words of their mothers, saying: We do not doubt our mothers knew it.	*Mothers are in a unique and God-given role to teach their children like no other can. The influence of a mother upon her children will reach into the eternities. Outsourcing the role of mother might bring costly consequences. Therefore, careful and prayerful consideration is recommended. It must be remembered that some situations leave little choice and thus merit no guilt or self-deprecation.*

Answer: **Alma 57:19–21**	Commentary:
19 But behold, my little band of two thousand and sixty fought most desperately; yea, they were firm before the Lamanites, and did administer death unto all those who opposed them.	*Helaman recounts his inspiring experience with the 2,060 young sons of the Anti-Nephi-Lehi converts who had fought with valor and courage in relieving the siege upon the army of Antipus.* *He was impressed with the character and obedient natures of these young men.*
20 And as the remainder of our army were about to give way before the Lamanites, behold, those two thousand and sixty were firm and undaunted.	*He describes how their level of obedience was ascribed to how they had been taught by their mothers.*

21 Yea, and they did obey and observe to perform every word of command with exactness; yea, and even according to their faith it was done unto them; and I did remember the words which they said unto me that their mothers had taught them.

There are many secular studies that show the great influence of a mother upon her children. Prophets have counseled and reminded mothers of their divine roles to influence. However, mothers must prayerfully study their individual circumstances and choose, as wisely as they can, how best to answer the question of working outside the home versus being a stay-at-home parent.

QUESTION 36

Why do Latter-day Saints have baptism and other ordinances for those who are dead?

Answer: **2 Nephi 9:23–24**	Commentary:
23 And he commandeth all men that they must repent, and be baptized in his name, having perfect faith in the Holy One of Israel, or they cannot be saved in the kingdom of God.	*The Lord clearly commanded that all should repent and be baptized in His name. If not, then salvation at its highest level cannot be attained.*
24 And if they will not repent and believe in his name, and be baptized in his name, and endure to the end, they must be damned; for the Lord God, the Holy One of Israel, has spoken it.	*Without the physical ordinance of baptism, progress is damned. Baptism and other saving ordinances are performed in the temple.*
	Mormons believe in life after death. Repentance and spiritual change after death can be accomplished. However, baptism and other physical ordinances can only be accomplished in this earthly realm. Mormon doctrine allows for worthy persons on earth to perform, by proxy, the observance of these important earthly steps.

	Agency is a fundamental part of Heavenly Father's Plan, therefore proxy ordinances do not obligate those deceased. It provides a service that allows them to accept or reject.

Answer: **3 Nephi 11:38**	Commentary:
38 And again I say unto you, ye must repent, and be baptized in my name, and become as a little child, or ye can in nowise inherit the kingdom of God.	*Christ commanded that entrance into the kingdom of God is predicated upon baptism, which is an earthly ordinance.*

Answer: **2 Nephi 31:17–18**	Commentary:
17 Wherefore, do the things which I have told you I have seen that your Lord and your Redeemer should do; for, for this cause have they been shown unto me, that ye might know the gate by which ye should enter. For the gate by which ye should enter is repentance and baptism by water; and then cometh a remission of your sins by fire and by the Holy Ghost. 18 And then are ye in this strait and narrow path which leads to eternal life; yea, ye have entered in by the gate; ye have done according to the commandments of the Father and the Son; and ye have received the Holy Ghost, which witnesses of	*Baptism and the reception of the Holy Ghost are requisite for entrance into God's kingdom. Therefore, every person who passes through earthly life and desires to be saved in the kingdom of God must be baptized. Perhaps commentary by prophets can also help:* *President Hinckley said, "Some wonder about who is directing the Church. I give you my solemn testimony that inspiration from on high is received and that it is our Father in Heaven and His Beloved Son, the Redeemer of the world, who are guiding and directing this church to bring to pass their eternal purposes in behalf of the sons and daughters of God."* (Gordon B. Hinckley, "Rejoice in this Great Era of Temple Building," general conference, Oct. 1985.)

the Father and the Son, unto the fulfilling of the promise which he hath made, that if ye entered in by the way ye should receive.

Elder D. Todd Christofferson said, "Some have misunderstood and suppose that deceased souls 'are being baptised into the Mormon faith without their knowledge' or that 'people who once belonged to other faiths can have the Mormon faith retroactively imposed on them.' They assume that we somehow have power to force a soul in matters of faith. Of course, we do not. God gave man his agency from the beginning. 'The dead who repent will be redeemed, through obedience to the ordinances of the house of God,' but only if they accept those ordinances." (D. Todd Christopherson, "The Redemption of the Dead and the Testimony of Jesus," general conference, Oct. 2000.)

QUESTION 37

How can I protect my family from the evils of the world?

Answer: **Helaman 5:9–12**

9 O remember, remember, my sons, the words which king Benjamin spake unto his people; yea, re member that there is no other way nor means whereby man can be saved, only through the atoning blood of Jesus Christ, who shall come; yea, remember that he com eth to redeem the world.

10 And remember also the words which Amulek spake unto Zeezrom, in the city of Ammonihah; for he said unto him that the Lord surely should come to redeem his people, but that he should not come to redeem them in their sins, but to redeem them from their sins.

Commentary:

Protecting our families from the evil of the world seems like an almost impossible task. We cannot adequately shield them from worldly influences while living in it. To isolate them from "the world" is also not feasible. Our best protection is to ensure they understand that Jesus Christ, the Son of God, came to atone for evil. The life focused on Him and His will is the one that will be protected from evil.

Our children should also know that the Savior has the capacity to redeem us from our sins, but will not save us in our sins. He will bless us as we seek Him!

11 And he hath power given unto him from the Father to redeem them from their sins because of repentance; therefore he hath sent his angels to declare the tidings of the conditions of repentance, which bringeth unto the power of the Redeemer, unto the salvation of their souls.	*We must teach that repentance is not an event but a lifestyle. To repent is to be in a constant effort to change and "put off the natural man or woman" and "become saints." The power of the Savior to keep us pure and liberated from sin is conditional upon our repentance and daily effort to live right.*
12 And now, my sons, remember, remember that it is upon the rock of our Redeemer, who is Christ, the Son of God, that ye must build your foundation; that when the devil shall send forth his mighty winds, yea, his shafts in the whirlwind, yea, when all his hail and his mighty storm shall beat upon you, it shall have no power over you to drag you down to the gulf of misery and endless wo, because of the rock upon which ye are built, which is a sure foundation, a foundation whereon if men build they cannot fall.	*"To remember" is "to be mindful of, to retain, and to learn by heart." We must teach our children to be mindful of and to retain the understanding that they must build their lives on the rock of Christ, the Son of God.* *Remembering is our greatest tool in overcoming the influence of Satan. The Savior's power is always stronger than the influence and power of Satan.* *Remembering Christ will discount any power Satan might exert.*

Answer: **Moroni 8:2–3**	Commentary:
2 My beloved son, Moroni, I rejoice exceedingly that your Lord Jesus Christ hath been mindful of you, and hath called you to his ministry, and to his holy work. 3 I am mindful of you always in my prayers, continually praying unto God the Father in the name of his	*In a letter written by Mormon to his son Moroni, he taught that Christ was very aware of him. Children need to know that they have not only earthly parents who are concerned for their well-being, but also a Father in Heaven, His Son Jesus Christ, and the Holy Ghost who love and desire their well being.*

Holy Child, Jesus, that he, through his infinite goodness and grace, will keep you through the endurance of faith on his name to the end.

Mormon expresses his own love for Moroni by telling him, "I am mindful of you always in my prayers." Great parents raise their children in large measure on their knees! They communicate love and concern for their children by helping them to understand that they pray for them always, asking the blessings of God to be upon them and always in their always.

QUESTION 38

How can I find peace, joy, and happiness in life?

Answer: **1 Nephi 8:10–12**	Commentary:
10 And it came to pass that I beheld a tree, whose fruit was desirable to make one happy. 11 And it came to pass that I did go forth and partake of the fruit thereof; and I beheld that it was most sweet, above all that I ever before tasted. Yea, and I beheld that the fruit thereof was white, to exceed all the whiteness that I had ever seen. 12 And as I partook of the fruit thereof it filled my soul with exceedingly great joy; wherefore, I began to be desirous that my family	*Happiness is the object and design of our existence. Everyone seeks to be happy! Human beings try many things to feel it. Most attempts bring fleeting and unsustainable spurts of happiness or a counterfeit rush. Drugs, pursuit of riches, sexual relationships, and other attempts to get a thrill are evidence of our desire for happiness.* *The fruit of the Tree of Life, as seen in Lehi's dream, is the Atonement of Jesus Christ. Nephi learned that the fruit "was desirable to make one happy." In other words, the fruit met mankind's natural desire for happiness. By partaking of the fruit, Lehi not only felt happy, but also*

should partake of it also; for I knew that it was desirable above all other fruit.	*experienced a higher sense of the satisfaction that we call "joy." Immediately, Lehi desired that his family feel and bask in it as well.* *The answer to this quest for happiness is in the Atonement of Jesus Christ.*

Answer: **Mosiah 2:41**	Commentary:
41 And moreover, I would desire that ye should consider on the blessed and happy state of those that keep the commandments of God. For behold, they are blessed in all things, both temporal and spiritual; and if they hold out faithful to the end they are received into heaven, that thereby they may dwell with God in a state of never-ending happiness. O remember, remember that these things are true; for the Lord God hath spoken it.	*Happiness comes to those who accept God and Christ and keep the commandments. Living in accordance with divine principles brings happiness. Anything against those principles might bring short-term counterfeits, but never sustainable happiness and joy.* *It isn't any more difficult than that. God has spoken it, and it is true.*

Answer: **2 Nephi 2:11, 13, 23, 24–25**	Commentary:
11 For it must needs be, that there is an opposition in all things. If not so, my first-born in the wilderness, righteousness could not be brought to pass, neither wickedness, neither holiness nor misery, neither good nor bad. Wherefore, all things must needs be a compound in one; wherefore, if it should be one body it must needs remain as dead, having no life	*Interestingly, Heavenly Father's great Plan of Happiness includes opposition, misery, death, and so on. Part of being happy is understanding the role of misery. Righteousness exists because there is wickedness. Good is what it is because of bad.* *There would be no sin without laws to compromise or commandments to be*

neither death, nor corruption nor incorruption, happiness nor misery, neither sense nor insensibility.

13 And if ye shall say there is no law, ye shall also say there is no sin. If ye shall say there is no sin, ye shall also say there is no righteousness. And if there be no righteousness there be no happiness. And if there be no righteousness nor happiness there be no punishment nor misery. And if these things are not there is no God. And if there is no God we are not, neither the earth; for there could have been no creation of things, neither to act nor to be acted upon; wherefore, all things must have vanished away.

23 And they would have had no children; wherefore they would have remained in a state of innocence, having no joy, for they knew no misery; doing no good, for they knew no sin.

24 But behold, all things have been done in the wisdom of him who knoweth all things.

25 Adam fell that men might be; and men are, that they might have joy.

broken, and, therefore, there would be no righteousness.

If you take away one, you take away the other. Ultimately, you take away God.

Happiness and joy can be the result of thorns, thistles, pernicious weeds, and all other effects of the Fall of life. If there had been no Fall, then there would be no need for an Atonement, hence neither progress nor growth. Everything would have been for naught.

Happiness springs from the Atonement— the Fruit of the Tree.

Without the Fall, Adam and Eve would never have experienced the challenges of mortality. They would have been innocent, without a knowledge of good and evil or misery and happiness. They would not have had children. They would never have known the greatest grief of having wicked children or the absolute pure joy that comes from a righteous posterity.

Answer: **Alma 5:14–34**

14 And now behold, I ask of you, my brethren of the church, have ye spiritually been born of God? Have ye received his image in your countenances? Have ye experienced this mighty change in your hearts?

15 Do ye exercise faith in the redemption of him who created you? Do you look forward with an eye of faith, and view this mortal body raised in immortality, and this corruption raised in incorruption, to stand before God to be judged according to the deeds which have been done in the mortal body?

16 I say unto you, can you imagine to yourselves that ye hear the voice of the Lord, saying unto you, in that day: Come unto me ye blessed, for behold, your works have been the works of righteousness upon the face of the earth?

17 Or do ye imagine to yourselves that ye can lie unto the Lord in that day, and say—Lord, our works have been righteous works upon the face of the earth—and that he will save you?

18 Or otherwise, can ye imagine yourselves brought before the tribunal of God with your souls filled with guilt and remorse, having a

Commentary:

In life, peace, joy, and happiness come as one lives according to the great Plan of Happiness designed by our Heavenly Father. It is the plan that will bring sustainable, lasting, even eternal happiness.

There is no other way! All else will ultimately evaporate.

In this chapter, Alma provides what can be considered a "checklist interview" to determine whether we are on the path that will get us safely to the Tree of Life to partake of the Fruit (Atonement).

As we read and digest each of the twenty questions asked by Alma, we can experience a sense of self examination. The extent to which we appropriately answer these questions will, in large measure, determine whether we are on the path that leads to the Tree, at which we can partake of the fruit and have "happiness, joy, and peace."

It would be appropriate to take notes as we review the balance of the questions to verse 31 and evaluate.

remembrance of all your guilt, yea, a perfect remembrance of all your wickedness, yea, a remembrance that ye have set at defiance the commandments of God?

19 I say unto you, can ye look up to God at that day with a pure heart and clean hands? I say unto you, can you look up, having the image of God engraven upon your countenances?

20 I say unto you, can ye think of being saved when you have yielded yourselves to become subjects to the devil?

21 I say unto you, ye will know at that day that ye cannot be saved; for there can no man be saved except his garments are washed white; yea, his garments must be purified until they are cleansed from all stain, through the blood of him of whom it has been spoken by our fathers, who should come to redeem his people from their sins.

22 And now I ask of you, my brethren, how will any of you feel, if ye shall stand before the bar of God, having your garments stained with blood and all manner of filthiness? Behold, what will these things testify against you?

23 Behold will they not testify that ye are murderers, yea, and also that ye are guilty of all manner of wickedness?

24 Behold, my brethren, do ye suppose that such an one can have a place to sit down in the kingdom of God, with Abraham, with Isaac, and with Jacob, and also all the holy prophets, whose garments are cleansed and are spotless, pure and white?

26 And now behold, I say unto you, my brethren, if ye have ex perienced a change of heart, and if ye have felt to sing the song of redeeming love, I would ask, can ye feel so now?

27 Have ye walked, keeping your- selves blameless before God? Could ye say, if ye were called to die at this time, within yourselves, that ye have been sufficiently humble? That your garments have been cleansed and made white through the blood of Christ, who will come to redeem his people from their sins?

28 Behold, are ye stripped of pride? I say unto you, if ye are not ye are not prepared to meet God. Behold ye must prepare quickly; for the kingdom of heaven is soon at hand, and such an one hath not eternal life.

29 Behold, I say, is there one among you who is not stripped of envy? I say unto you that such an one is not prepared; and I would that he should prepare quickly, for the hour is close at hand, and he knoweth not when the time shall come; for such an one is not found guiltless.

30 And again I say unto you, is there one among you that doth make a mock of his brother, or that heapeth upon him persecutions?

31 Wo unto such an one, for he is not prepared, and the time is at hand that he must repent or he cannot be saved!

32 Yea, even wo unto all ye workers of iniquity; repent, repent, for the Lord God hath spoken it!

33 Behold, he sendeth an invitation unto all men, for the arms of mercy are extended towards them, and he saith: Repent, and I will receive you.

34 Yea, he saith: Come unto me and ye shall partake of the fruit of the tree of life; yea, ye shall eat and drink of the bread and the waters of life freely;

As the "interview" questions conclude, Alma states with clarity that we must repent. We must change and live our lives in accordance with the questions asked.

"Iniquity" is defined as "having a lack of righteous focus." Alma states that those "having a lack of righteous focus" need to change and center their attention on that which God has designed to give us sustainable, eternal joy and happiness.

He testifies of the love and arms of mercy extended to all who will repent and change.

Happiness, peace, and joy come to those who partake of the Atonement and receive the Savior and His sustaining love.

QUESTION 39
Why should I keep a journal?

Answer: **Jacob 1:2–4**	Commentary:
2 And he gave me, Jacob, a commandment that I should write upon these plates a few of the things which I considered to be most precious; that I should not touch, save it were lightly, concerning the history of this people which are called the people of Nephi.	*God gave a commandment to Jacob and all other prophets to preserve a record for future generations. He asked that the most important things be recorded, to the end that future generations could be blessed with revelations, teachings, and experiences. Those insights have blessed countless numbers of people.*
3 For he said that the history of his people should be engraven upon his other plates, and that I should preserve these plates and hand them down unto my seed, from generation to generation.	*In a similar way, members of the Church have been counseled to maintain journals—to record feelings, experiences, and personal insights gained while traveling through life. This personal history can indeed help those who follow, not only to know us, but also to apply what we learned in their own lives' journeys. A diary is*
4 And if there were preaching which was sacred, or revelation	

which was great, or prophesying, that I should engraven the heads of them upon these plates, and touch upon them as much as it were possible, for Christ's sake, and for the sake of our people.	*a day-to-day logbook of what we do. A journal is more. In it we record feelings, learnings, and experiences that help us to see more clearly. Jacob was counseled to touch only "lightly" on diary information and was commanded to write those things that were "most precious" instead.*

Answer: **Alma 37:2–4**	Commentary:
2 And I also command you that ye keep a record of this people, according as I have done, upon the plates of Nephi, and keep all these things sacred which I have kept, even as I have kept them; for it is for a wise purpose that they are kept.	*Commandments are given by Heavenly Father to bless His children. Sometimes we must trust our Father in Heaven—trust that in His omniscience he commands for "a wise purpose." Perhaps our journaling will bless us or someone else in the future.*
3 And these plates of brass, which contain these engravings, which have the records of the holy scriptures upon them, which have the genealogy of our forefathers, even from the beginning—	*Recording about our lives and how we are connected to past generations fulfills a yearning that nearly everyone has. Recording our ancestry connections will bless and help link those in future generations to those of the past.*
4 Behold, it has been prophesied by our fathers, that they should be kept and handed down from one generation to another, and be kept and preserved by the hand of the Lord until they should go forth unto every nation, kindred, tongue, and people, that they shall know of the mysteries contained thereon.	*Journals bless those in the future and are therapeutic to the writer. Something interesting happens when we seek to crystallize our thoughts and feelings in the written word. Writing solidifies feelings and helps the writer to see things more clearly.*

Answer: **Helaman 3:13–15**

13 And now there are many records kept of the proceedings of this people, by many of this people, which are particular and very large, concerning them.

14 But behold, a hundredth part of the proceedings of this people, yea, the account of the Lamanites and of the Nephites, and their wars, and contentions, and dissensions, and their preaching, and their prophecies, and their shipping and their building of ships, and their building of temples, and of synagogues and their sanctuaries, and their righteousness, and their wickedness, and their murders, and their robbings, and their plundering, and all manner of abominations and whoredoms, cannot be contained in this work.

15 But behold, there are many books and many records of every kind, and they have been kept chiefly by the Nephites.

Commentary:

This scripture helps us to see that, over time, the Nephite library became something very significant. It contained writings on nearly every subject, including war, peace, temple building, and even the construction of ships.

Each volume of a prophet's writings became an important part of a larger library. This collection became a critical element in helping the Nephites to remember who they were. Remembering helped them to turn to God. It was when they forgot that they went through cycles of pride and were ultimately destroyed.

Writing, journaling, recording, and reviewing help future generations to remember.

QUESTION 40
Why is the law of chastity so important?

Answer: Jacob 2:7

7 And also it grieveth me that I must use so much boldness of speech concerning you, before your wives and your children, many of whose feelings are exceedingly tender and chaste and delicate before God, which thing is pleasing unto God;

Commentary:

Jacob taught that the issue of chastity is something tender and delicate to righteous, innocent women and children. The need to be bold in his discussion with men is evidence that chastity is pleasing to God. Anything that crosses the line, is contrary to it, or makes light of it, is to be abhorred.

Answer: **Jacob 2:28**	Commentary:
28 For I, the Lord God, delight in the chastity of women. And whoredoms are an abomination before me; thus saith the Lord of Hosts.	*Chastity and cleanliness are special subjects that delight Heavenly Father. Whoredoms, or sexual sin, contradict the sanctity of giving life to His children. Disgust and sadness replace adoration, love, and joy when the beauty and sanctity of sex is tread upon in any degree of unholiness.*

Answer: **Alma 39:5**	Commentary:
5 Know ye not, my son, that these things are an abomination in the sight of the Lord; yea, most abominable above all sins save it be the shedding of innocent blood or denying the Holy Ghost?	*Corianton violated the law of chastity. Alma reminded him that sexual sin is an atrocity. It disgraces the gift that God gives His children to participate in giving life to His spirit children. Adultery, fornication, or anything like it is given the classification of being very serious in the eyes of God.* *Forgiveness is possible. The seriousness of sexual sin requires time to repent properly. It requires Godly sorrow and evidence that complete change, or turning away has been completed.*

Answer: **1 Nephi 10:21**	Commentary:
21 Wherefore, if ye have sought to do wickedly in the days of your probation, then ye are found unclean before the judgment-seat of God; and no unclean thing can dwell with God; wherefore, ye must be cast off forever.	*To be "clean" is to be "virtuous, good, moral, pure, chaste, and innocent."* *To be "unclean" is to be "impure, forbidden, or dirty."* *The objective to remain clean, or to become clean, is one of the most important things we can do to return to Heavenly Father.*

Answer: **Alma 7:21**	Commentary:
21 And he doth not dwell in unholy temples; neither can filthiness or anything which is unclean be received into the kingdom of God; therefore I say unto you the time shall come, yea, and it shall be at the last day, that he who is filthy shall remain in his filthiness.	*Being clean is a requirement for having the Spirit with us and for being qualified to attain the kingdom of God. Working to be cleansed of our natural fallen state of being is the great objective of life on earth.*

Answer: **Mormon 9:28**	Commentary:
28 Be wise in the days of your probation; strip yourselves of all uncleanness; ask not, that ye may consume it on your lusts, but ask with a firmness unshaken, that ye will yield to no temptation, but that ye will serve the true and living God.	*Moroni calls upon us to become clean and strip ourselves of anything that might soil or stain our capacity to live worthy of the Holy Ghost. "Lusts"—one of the most insidious temptations utilized by Lucifer in his attempt to spoil our lives—is highlighted.*

QUESTION 41

How do we deal with a hyper conscience and the feeling that we are never worthy or good enough to please Heavenly Father and gain His favor?

Answer: **Mosiah 4:2–3**	Commentary:
2 And they had viewed themselves in their own carnal state, even less than the dust of the earth. And they all cried aloud with one voice, saying: O have mercy, and apply the atoning blood of Christ that we may receive forgiveness of our sins, and our hearts may be purified; for we believe in Jesus Christ, the Son of God, who created heaven and earth, and all things; who shall come down among the children of men.	*Having humility is essential to accepting and fully utilizing the Atonement in our lives. However, feeling that we are never worthy or able to rise to a level acceptable in the eyes of a loving and merciful Father in Heaven is counterproductive to our receiving the blessings that the Atonement provides.*
	Peace of conscience comes when we turn our faith completely and totally toward Christ. The Spirit of the Lord comes to us and gives us joy. We know that our sins are forgiven.
3 And it came to pass that after they had spoken these words the Spirit of the Lord came upon them, and they were filled with joy, having received a remission of their sins, and having peace of conscience,	*A hyper conscience discounts His power to give us peace. Faith in the Lord Jesus*

because of the exceeding faith which they had in Jesus Christ who should come, according to the words which king Benjamin had spoken unto them.	*Christ and His Atonement brings joy, peace, and a love for God.* *The answer to this question is in the first principle of the gospel—faith in the Lord Jesus Christ!*

Answer: **2 Nephi 22:2**	Commentary:
2 Behold, God is my salvation; I will trust, and not be afraid; for the Lord Jehovah is my strength and my song; he also has become my salvation.	*Trusting in God and focusing on Christ allows us to move our attention from ourselves and our weaknesses. He is our salvation! We cannot do it ourselves! He knows we are imperfect. His Atonement covers us when we do our best and keep trying.*

Answer: **Mosiah 26:29–30**	Commentary:
29 Therefore I say unto you, Go; and whosoever transgresseth against me, him shall ye judge according to the sins which he has committed; and if he confess his sins before thee and me, and repenteth in the sincerity of his heart, him shall ye forgive, and I will forgive him also. 30 Yea, and as often as my people repent will I forgive them their trespasses against me.	*Heavenly Father is a forgetting God. If we are sincere and we confess our sins, then He "remembers our sins no more."* *One with a hyper conscience might say, "But I keep sinning over and over again even though I try to repent and stop."* *Trust Father in Heaven, who loves us sufficiently enough that he promises to forgive us often in our quest to become as He is. Remember that the quest for perfection will never end here on earth.*

Answer: **2 Nephi 4:17–18, 26–28, 32–34**	Commentary:

17 Nevertheless, notwithstanding the great goodness of the Lord, in showing me his great and marvelous works, my heart exclaimeth: O wretched man that I am! Yea, my heart sorroweth because of my flesh; my soul grieveth because of mine iniquities.

Just after the death of Lehi, Nephi wrote of feelings of unworthiness and lack of capability. It is not unusual for the spiritually sensitive to feel that. He used the word "wretched" to describe his sorrow and grief. It seems that he felt overcome by his inquity, or lack of righteous focus.

18 I am encompassed about, because of the temptations and the sins which do so easily beset me.

To highlight just a few of its synonyms, "wretchedness" is a strong word meaning "dejected, depressed, despicable, shameful, cursed, rotten, lousy, scummy, and even damned."

26 O then, if I have seen so great things, if the Lord in his con descension unto the children of men hath visited men in so much mercy, why should my heart weep and my soul linger in the valley of sorrow, and my flesh waste away, and my strength slacken, because of mine afflictions?

Apparently Nephi feels sinful and unable to deal with the temptations that beleaguer and afflict him. He feels hopelessly inadequate to enter the kingdom of God.

27 And why should I yield to sin, because of my flesh? Yea, why should I give way to temptations, that the evil one have place in my heart to destroy my peace and afflict my soul? Why am I angry because of mine enemy?

Ultimately, Nephi rebounds from his hyper conscience and his worry about unworthiness. He recognizes and re-members the blessing of Christ and His Atonement. He begins to highlight his blessings and the good things he's learned and accomplished.

28 Awake, my soul! No longer droop in sin. Rejoice, O my heart, and give place no more for the enemy of my soul.

He tells his sagging spirit to stop it and to cease to give up hope. He determines to kick the enemy of his soul out of his life and to refocus upon the Savior.

32 May the gates of hell be shut continually before me, because that my heart is broken and my spirit is contrite! O Lord, wilt thou not shut the gates of thy righteousness before me, that I may walk in the path of the low valley, that I may be strict in the plain road!	*He sees discouragement as a tool of Satan and vows to find strength in his testimony of the goodness and mercy of God.*
33 O Lord, wilt thou encircle me around in the robe of thy righteousness! O Lord, wilt thou make a way for mine escape before mine enemies! Wilt thou make my path straight before me! Wilt thou not place a stumbling block in my way —but that thou wouldst clear my way before me, and hedge not up my way, but the ways of mine enemy.	
34 O Lord, I have trusted in thee, and I will trust in thee forever. I will not put my trust in the arm of flesh; for I know that cursed is he that putteth his trust in the arm of flesh. Yea, cursed is he that putteth his trust in man or maketh flesh his arm.	*He replaces pessimism with optimism and trust in the Lord!* *He commits anew to remembering the power and purpose of God and the Savior in his life.*

Answer: **3 Nephi 18:18−19**	Commentary:
18 Behold, verily, verily, I say unto you, ye must watch and pray always lest ye enter into temptation; for Satan desireth to have you, that he may sift you as wheat.	*The most powerful connection with God is prayer. Lucifer understands that prayer is the key that brings our focus back to God.* *When prayer becomes weak and erratic,*

19 Therefore ye must always pray unto the Father in my name;	*so does the spirit of man. When prayer (formal and informal) is strong, so is the man.* *Pray always!*

Answer: **Mosiah 7:33**	Commentary:
33 But if ye will turn to the Lord with full purpose of heart, and put your trust in him, and serve him with all diligence of mind, if ye do this, he will, according to his own will and pleasure, deliver you out of bondage.	*When we are down on ourselves or feel inadequate, changing our focus from ourselves to Him will do wonders. Trust Him! Remember Him and His power to lift and nurture. His purpose is to lift, not to condemn. He requires diligent effort and a purposeful heart. He is far more merciful and forgiving than we can understand. He is also a very forgetting God. When we are trying our best, He remembers our inadequacies no more. That means that He forgets our sins. But we will not forget our sins. Remembering them helps us to remain humble and dependant on His mercy, which is good.*

Answer: **Moroni 10:33**	Commentary:
33 And again, if ye by the grace of God are perfect in Christ, and deny not his power, then are ye sanctified in Christ by the grace of God, through the shedding of the blood of Christ, which is in the covenant of the Father unto the remission of your sins, that ye become holy, without spot.	*The role of the Savior is to save! His function, through His grace, is to sanctify and magnify us.* *As we try with all our power, He, with His infinite power, makes us able.*

QUESTION 42

Why is obedience to commandments, mission rules, honor codes, city ordinances, and the laws of the land so important?

Answer: **Alma 57:21–22**	Commentary:
21 Yea, and they did obey and observe to perform every word of command with exactness; yea, and even according to their faith it was done unto them; and I did remember the words which they said unto me that their mothers had taught them.	*Honor and being true is the key to answering this question.*
	Obedience is the first law of heaven. It is primary to the covenants that we make in the temple. Obedience brings blessings.
22 And now behold, it was these my sons, and those men who had been selected to convey the prisoners, to whom we owe this great victory; for it was they who did beat the Lamanites; therefore they were driven back to the city of Manti.	*It is less about keeping a mission rule regarding the clock (getting up or going to bed at a certain time), dressing in accordance with university dress codes, driving slower in a school zone, or maintaining one's yard in conformity to community ordinances. It has more to do with our attitude toward obedience. Will we do what we promised we would do? When we are obedient to our commitments, we are blessed with power that comes through*

the Holy Ghost. When we agree to serve a mission for the Church, we agree to live by the rules set forth by those responsible for missionary work—the Apostles. When we sign a campus honor or dress code, we agree to behave accordingly. When we obtain the privilege of driving a vehicle, we agree to abide by traffic rules. When we buy property in certain city boundaries, we agree to certain covenants, conditions, and restrictions that pertain to that property.

Living in accordance with what we've agreed to do brings power into our lives. Being selectively obedient or doing what we want instead of what we should do, weakens our character. Worst of all, it offends the Spirit of the Holy Ghost.

Answer: 1 Nephi 3:7

7 And it came to pass that I, Nephi, said unto my father: I will go and do the things which the Lord hath commanded, for I know that the Lord giveth no commandments unto the children of men, save he shall prepare a way for them that they may accomplish the thing which he commandeth them.

Commentary:

Obedience is an attitude. Nephi tells his father Lehi that he will obey the Lord and His commandments. He does not equivocate! He doesn't say he'll try. He clearly states that if God commands, then He will do what he is asked. He trusts that God has His reasons, and that is sufficient.

QUESTION 43
Why is the way we look or dress so important?

Answer: All of Alma 2 for background and **Alma 3**, with specific focus on following verses

4 And the Amlicites were distinguished from the Nephites, for they had marked themselves with red in their foreheads after the manner of the Lamanites; nevertheless

Commentary:

The Amlicites were a group of apostate Nephites who joined with the Lamanites to battle against their own people. Lamanites had darker skin color than the Nephites had. In war, this difference served both sides equally well. Hand-to-hand combat was more easily executed when one could determine the enemy by skin color.

However, when the light-skinned Amlicites joined forces with the dark-skinned Lamanites, there was a problem. The enemy was not able to be identified by skin color.

To solve this problem, the Amilicites "marked themselves" with red on their foreheads. This was done for the obvious

they had not shorn their heads like unto the Lamanites.

13 Now we will return again to the Amlicites, for they also had a mark set upon them; yea, they set the mark upon themselves, yea, even a mark of red upon their foreheads.

19 Now I would that ye should see that they brought upon themselves the curse; and even so doth every man that is cursed bring upon himself his own condemnation.

purpose of identifying themselves with the Lamanites whom they had joined.

Mormon explains that every man marks himself in a way that will bless him or associate him with evil.

Our dress, how we groom, and what we do to our bodies (tattoos, piercings, and so on) mark us.

At a glance or in an instance, our dress or hairstyle can reflect whether or not we associate with skaters, athletes, or homosexuals. We can communicate with our clothing and hairstyle that we are the Lord's missionaries. Stud piercings in the lips or nose, multiple piercings in our ears, or a tattoo on our neck or body can indicate we don't listen to or care about what prophets have counseled. In seconds, our appearance identifies us with a certain culture or lifestyle.

Appearance is important. Missionaries would do well to dress and groom their hair in a standard like that of our church leaders, being careful not to mark themselves as representing anyone but the Lord.

How a woman wears her blouse, pants, or skirt can quickly mark her for good or cause questions about her commitment or intentions. The same applies to men who mark themselves by their style.

All of us should take stock in how we are marking ourselves and make sure it reflects discipleship of the Savior.

QUESTION 44

What are my responsibilities in the lineage of Joseph, and how should they influence my decisions in life?

Answer: **3 Nephi 21:13–16**	Commentary:
	Salt was a token of the covenant. Why salt? What are the properties that make salt an ideal token of the covenant (or symbol) of this important group of people?
13 Verily, verily, I say unto you, I give unto you to be the salt of the earth; but if the salt shall lose its savor wherewith shall the earth be salted? The salt shall be thenceforth good for nothing, but to be cast out and to be trodden under foot of men.	*Salt preserves, cleanses, purifies, and gives life. Human beings cannot live without it. It preserves food. It cleanses wounds. Anciently, pure salt was of great value because of the foregoing reasons. However, if salt becomes rancid—or if it becomes impure (lose its savor)—it has no value.* *Therefore, when Jesus was speaking, He directed His counsel to the salt, or the covenant people. He indicated that if the salt or covenant people, didn't fulfil their*

14 Verily, verily, I say unto you, I give unto you to be the light of this people. A city that is set on a hill cannot be hid.

15 Behold, do men light a candle and put it under a bushel? Nay, but on a candlestick, and it giveth light to all that are in the house;

16 Therefore let your light so shine before this people, that they may see your good works and glorify your Father who is in heaven.

role, they weren't worth much except to be trodden under the foot of men (or beast) in the streets of Jerusalem.

Just days prior to Jesus's teaching the Nephites, He was in Jerusalem. Early in the morning, the street sweepers would have come into the streets to clean from the previous day in preparation for the coming day. They would have swept up the animal dung and refuse and deposited it in baskets (just as they would have done every other day). They would have taken the baskets to "Dung Gate," where they would have left it for the garbage collectors to transport it out to the city dump. The collectors would have dumped the baskets of mostly dung, fruit pits, peelings, and other refuse. The hot sun would have dried out the fresh dung, and the garbage dump would have controlled the volume and quantity of the trash by burning it. The dump was often referred to as the "Lake of Fire and Brimstone." At the garbage dump, or "dung hill," the fire burned continually.

Interestingly, fire, according to university chemists, burns out the impurities and returns it to clean salt.

Speaking to the "salt of the earth" or the covenant people, Christ reminds us that we must be a light to the rest of the house (of Israel). He commands that the salt must let their light shine, or their value in the grand scheme of things will be minimal. Their purpose is diminished,

	and only through the heat of proper repentance and forgiveness can they return again to fulfill their role.
	Children of the covenant have a very important purpose: it is to position ourselves through quiet example and righteousness to give light—to assist in purifying, cleansing, and healing a sick and broken world.

Answer: **Alma 46:12–24,** with specific focus on the following verses	Commentary:
23 Moroni said unto them: Behold, we are a remnant of the seed of Jacob; yea, we are a remnant of the seed of Joseph, whose coat was rent by his brethren into many pieces; yea, and now behold, let us remember to keep the commandments of God, or our garments shall be rent by our brethren, and we be cast into prison, or be sold, or be slain.	*Captain Moroni created the Title of Liberty. This caused his people to recalculate their orientation and understand their purpose.* *First they were to focus on their memory of God, religion, freedom, peace, wives, and children.* *Then he helped them understand that their true mission was not a battle against the Lamanites, but, more important, that they were to focus on their covenants and keep them. He compared them to their great-great grandfather, Joseph, and his purpose.*
24 Yea, let us preserve our liberty as a remnant of Joseph; yea, let us remember the words of Jacob, before his death, for behold, he saw that a part of the remnant of the coat of Joseph was preserved and had not decayed. And he said— Even as this remnant of garment of my son hath been preserved, so shall a remnant of the seed of my son be preserved by the hand of God, and	*Joseph was a "savior of men." He preserved his family (the House of Israel). The gospel he taught cleansed and purified. Life was given to the world through the light and life of Christ.*

be taken unto himself, while the remainder of the seed of Joseph shall perish, even as the remnant of his garment.	

Answer: **3 Nephi 18:24**	Commentary:
24 Therefore, hold up your light that it may shine unto the world. Behold I am the light which ye shall hold up—that which ye have seen me do. Behold ye see that I have prayed unto the Father, and ye all have witnessed.	*The Savior reminds us all that we should not only be a light unto the world but also remember that He, Jesus Christ, is the light.* *Our decisions and directions in life should constantly toward our Savior, if we hope to be true Christians. We hold Him up as the light. As Joseph saved his family, we too can provide the light of the Savior to all around us. We can be saviors of men.*

CONCLUSION

We have explored many "questions of the soul" in this book. The intent was never to present an exhaustive list of every question of the soul. Neither would it be possible to give all answers to each of life's vexing questions. We have explored questions and found answers within the pages of the Book of Mormon. A deliberate effort was made to keep the answers simple and straightforward. The intent has been to maintain a focus on scriptural content and to avoid any attempt to give deep or interpretive answers. It is likely that, as you have studied the questions posed herein, you have thought, "Oh, but what about the story of _____? The author should have included it too!" It is by design that every possible answer and angle has not been given. Rather, an invitation is extended to find your own answers and to study additional questions.

Following these concluding thoughts, additional pages are provided in the same format as the rest of the book's whereon you may add more questions and search for more answers. I now step out of the study we have conducted together. It is intended that this be the beginning of your book—not the end. Study, search, and enjoy your continuing effort to identify answers to the questions of the soul from the Book of Mormon.

It is my testimony that the Book of Mormon is the word of God. It provides us with clarifying perspective to the Bible teachings, but it never detracts from the beauty of biblical doctrine. The Book of Mormon is the greatest handbook for living, providing insight and understanding as we move through this life. As its translator once testified, "I told the brethren that the Book of Mormon was the most correct of any book on the earth, and the keystone of our religion, and a man would get nearer to God by abiding by its precepts, than by any other book" (Joseph Smith Jr.).

I give my personal testimony that the Book of Mormon has had such an impact in my life. With all my weaknesses and shortcomings, I am a better man, husband, father, servant, leader, teacher, student, and businessman for having the teachings of the Book of Mormon in my life. I testify that it is both true and convincingly helpful in giving insight and understanding to questions of the soul.

QUESTION:

_____

_____

_____

Answer:_____	Commentary:

QUESTION:

_____

_____

_____

Answer:_____	Commentary:

QUESTION:

_____

_____

_____

Answer:_____	Commentary:

QUESTION:

_____

_____

_____

Answer:_____

Commentary:

QUESTION:

_____

_____

_____

| Answer:_____ | Commentary: |
| | |

QUESTION:

_____

_____

Answer:_____	Commentary:

QUESTION:

_____

_____

_____

Answer:_____	Commentary:

QUESTION:

Answer:_____

Commentary: